Silver Burdett Ginn
Mathematics

THE PATH
TO MATH
SUCCESS!

Silver Burdett Ginn
Parsippany, NJ
Atlanta, GA • Deerfield, IL • Irving, TX • Needham, MA • Upland, CA

Program Authors

Francis (Skip) Fennell, Ph.D.
Professor of Education and Chair, Education Department

Western Maryland College
Westminster, Maryland

Joan Ferrini-Mundy, Ph.D.
Professor of Mathematics

University of New Hampshire
Durham, New Hampshire

Herbert P. Ginsburg, Ph.D.
Professor of Psychology and Mathematics Education

Teachers College, Columbia University
New York, New York

Carole Greenes, Ed.D.
Professor of Mathematics Education and Associate Dean,
 School of Education

Boston University
Boston, Massachusetts

Stuart J. Murphy
Visual Learning Specialist

Evanston, Illinois

William Tate, Ph.D.
Associate Professor of Mathematics Education

University of Wisconsin-Madison
Madison, Wisconsin

ISBN 0-382-37984-5

2 3 4 5 6 7 8 9 10 GB 05 04 03 02 01 00 99

Grade Level Authors

Mary Behr Altieri, M.S.
Mathematics Teacher
1993 Presidential Awardee
Lakeland Central School District
Shrub Oak, New York

Jennie Bennett, Ed.D.
Instructional Mathematics Supervisor
Houston Independent School District
Houston, Texas

Charles Calhoun, Ph.D.
Associate Professor of Elementary
  Education (Mathematics)
University of Alabama at Birmingham
Birmingham, Alabama

Lucille Croom, Ph.D.
Professor of Mathematics
Hunter College of the City University
  of New York
New York, New York

Robert A. Laing, Ph.D.
Professor of Mathematics Education
Western Michigan University
Kalamazoo, Michigan

Kay B. Sammons, M.S.
Supervisor of Elementary Mathematics
Howard County Public Schools
Ellicott City, Maryland

Marian Small, Ed.D.
Professor of Mathematics Education
University of New Brunswick
Fredericton, New Brunswick, Canada

Contributing Authors

Stephen Krulik, Ed.D.
Professor of Mathematics Education
Temple University
Philadelphia, Pennsylvania

Donna J. Long
Mathematics/Title 1 Coordinator
Metropolitan School District of
  Wayne Township
Indianapolis, Indiana

Jesse A. Rudnick, Ed.D.
Professor Emeritus of Mathematics
  Education
Temple University
Philadelphia, Pennsylvania

Clementine Sherman
Director, USI Math and Science
Dade County Public Schools
Miami, Florida

Bruce R. Vogeli, Ph.D.
Clifford Brewster Upton Professor of
  Mathematics
Teachers College, Columbia University
New York, New York

Silver Burdett Ginn
A Division of Simon & Schuster
299 Jefferson Road, P.O. Box 480
Parsippany, NJ 07054-0480

iii

Contents

Sorting and Classifying

Chapter Theme: I'm a Kindergartner

Exploring Patterns

Chapter Theme: I'm a Nature Spy

Chapter 3

Exploring Numbers to 5

Chapter Theme: I'm a Friend

———— *Chapter Resources* ————

Chapter 4

Shapes and Sharing

Chapter Theme: I'm an Artist

———— *Chapter Resources* ————

Chapter 5

Exploring Numbers to 10

Chapter Theme: I'm a Cook

Chapter 6

Measurement

Chapter Theme: I'm a Builder

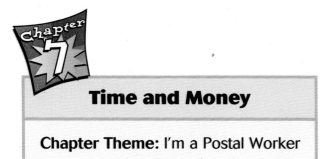

Time and Money

Chapter Theme: I'm a Postal Worker

———— *Chapter Resources* ————

Exploring Greater Numbers

Chapter Theme: I'm a Teacher

———— *Chapter Resources* ————

Chapter 9

Exploring Addition

Chapter Theme: I'm a Storyteller

Chapter 10

Exploring Subtraction

Chapter Theme: I'm a Farmer

CHAPTER 1

Sorting and Classifying

I'm a Kindergartner

A Note to the Family

During the next few weeks, your child will sort and classify things by position, color, shape, and size. Here are some learning ideas you can share together.

 At-Home Activities

- Have your child place a toy in various locations, such as
  - inside a drawer
  - outside a clothes hamper
  - to the left of a plant
  - to the right of a table
  - on a top, middle, or bottom shelf
- Sort clothes or toys together. Sort objects by color, size, and shape.
- Collect three different socks and a shirt. Have your child point to the object that doesn't belong. Ask him or her to describe how the shirt is different from the socks.

Read About It!

To read more with your child about sorting and classifying, look for these books in your local library.

- *Becca Backward, Becca Frontward: A Book of Concept Pairs* by Bruce McMillan (Lothrop, Lee & Shepard, 1986)
- *The Color Box* by Dayle A. Dodds (Little, Brown, 1992)
- *Outside, Inside* by Carolyn Crimi (Simon & Schuster, 1995)

A2

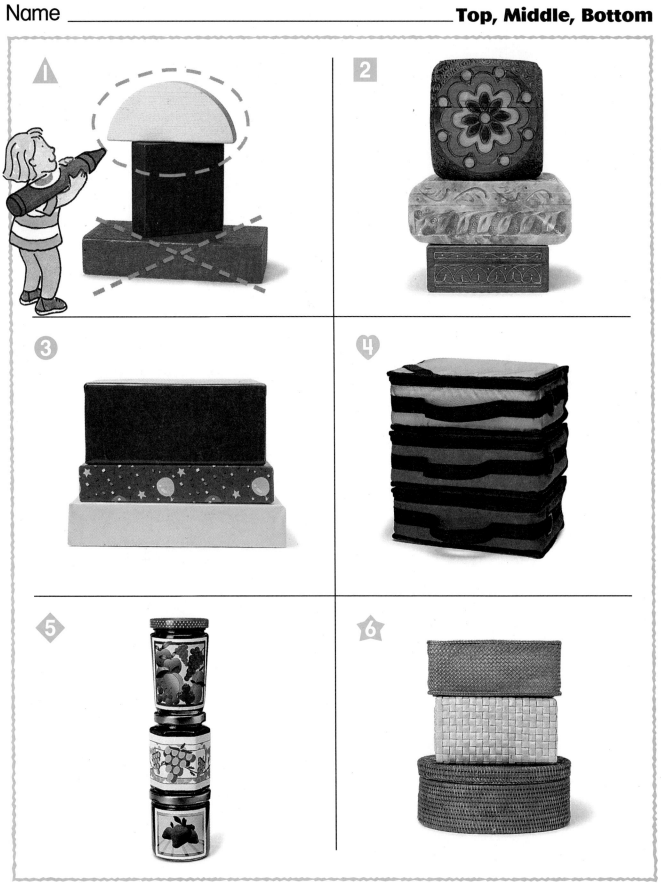

1

2

3

4

5

6

Directions Have children circle each top item and mark an *X* on each bottom item.

Home Connection Stack three books or boxes and ask your child to identify the top, middle, and bottom item.

Directions Have children circle each middle item and mark an X on each bottom item.

A4

Name _____

Over, Under, On

A5

Directions Have children cut out the pictures, then glue one picture over the table, one on the table, and one under the table.

Home Connection Ask your child to find some objects around your home that are over something and some that are under something.

Directions Have children glue one picture over the shelf, one on the shelf, and one under the shelf.

A6

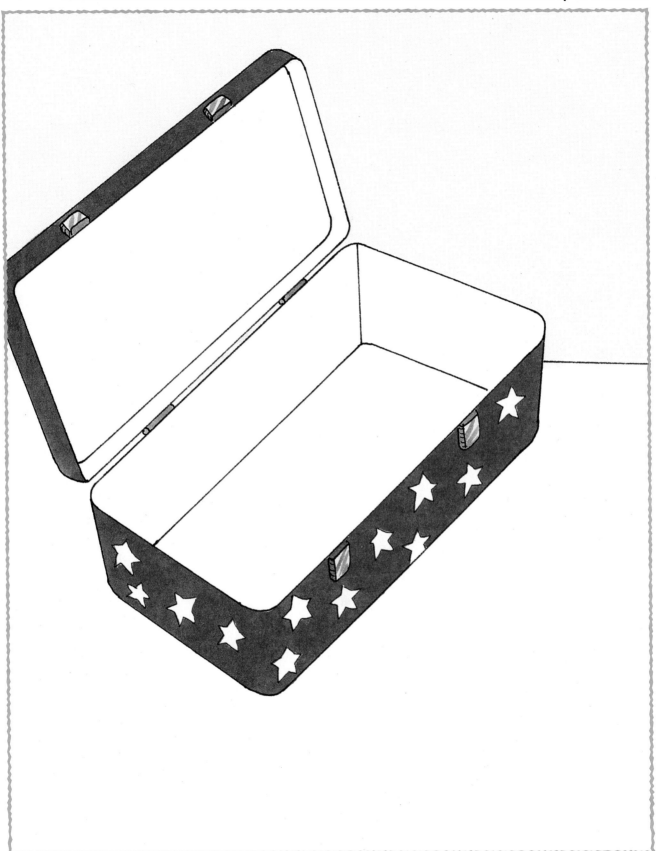

Directions Have children draw food and lunch items inside and outside the lunch box. Then have them circle the items that are inside the lunch box.

Home Connection Ask your child to collect items to put inside a bowl or box. Then have him or her place the same items outside the container.

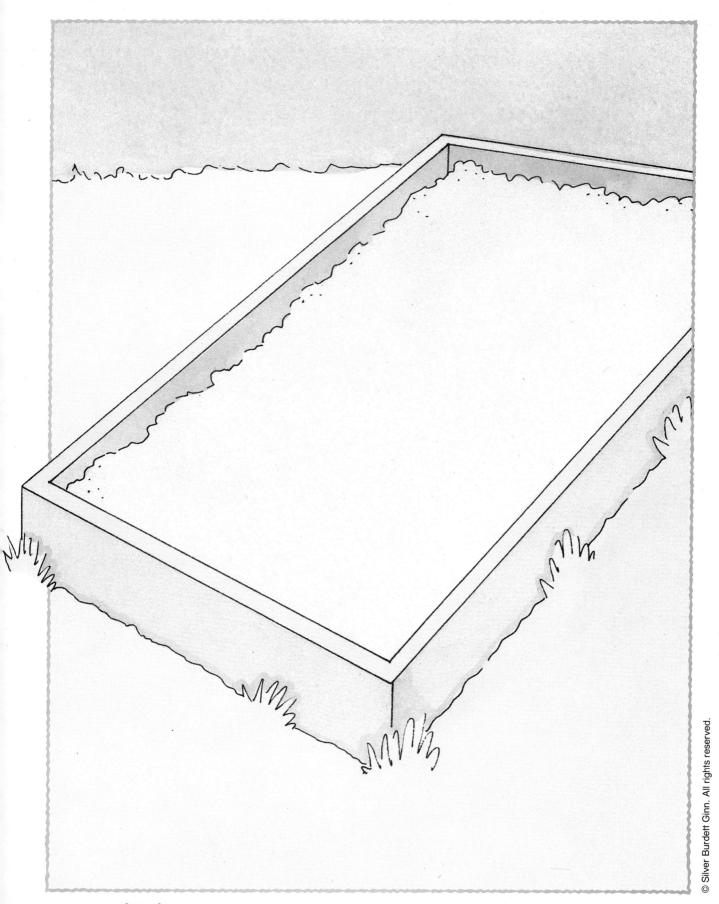

Directions Have children draw playground items and toys inside and outside the sandbox. Then have them circle the items that are outside the sandbox.

A8

Left

Right

Directions Have children place red counters in the left box and blue counters in the right box. Then have them draw the corresponding number of counters.

 Home Connection Ask your child to help you sort the laundry into two piles. Have him or her put shirts in a pile to the left and pants in a pile to the right.

Left   # Right

Directions Have children identify objects on the left and right side of
the playground. Ask them to draw a child on the left and a bird on the right.

A10

Directions Have children circle the two items in each row that are the same.

A11

Directions Have children circle the item in each row that is different from the other two items.

A12

Problem-Solving
Use Logical Reasoning
STRATEGY
Understand
Plan
Solve
Look Back

Name _____

1

2

3

4

Directions Have children mark an X on the object in each group that doesn't belong.

Home Connection Collect several socks and one shirt. Ask your child, "What doesn't belong in this pile? Why not?"

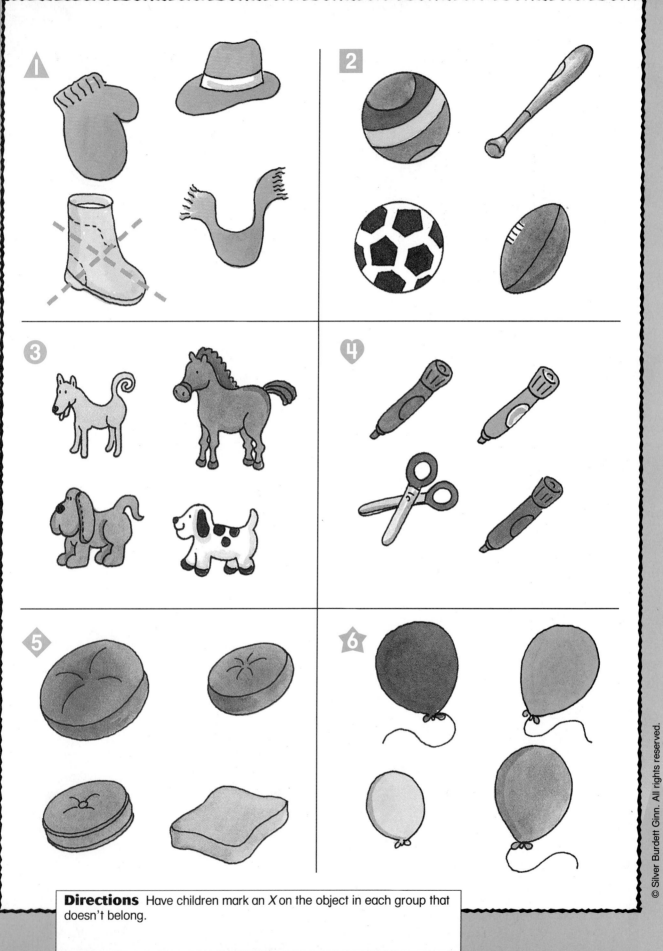

Directions Have children mark an X on the object in each group that doesn't belong.

A14

Name _____

Directions Have children: **1.** circle the middle item, **2.** circle the item that is under the table, **3.** circle the person outside the building, **4.** circle the person on the left, **5.** circle the dog that is different, and **6.** circle the object that doesn't belong.

Directions Challenge children to finish the picture. Encourage them to look at the rest of the picture for clues on how to complete it.

I'm a Nature Spy

A Note to the Family

During the next few weeks, your child will be learning about patterns. Here are some learning ideas you can share together.

At-Home Activities

- Take your child on a nature walk and collect various items, such as seeds, leaves, seashells, twigs, and pebbles. Ask your child to glue these objects onto a sheet of paper or cloth in a repeating pattern. For example, pine cone, leaf, pine cone, leaf, pine cone, leaf.

- If possible, collect leaves of different colors. Encourage your child to make another pattern, this time alternating colors. For example, red, red, yellow, red, red, yellow. This can also be done with other objects, such as buttons or pasta.

- Create a rhythm pattern with your child, such as snap-snap-clap, snap-snap-clap. Together you could give the pattern a special meaning, such as "It's time to wash your hands for dinner."

Read About It!

To read more with your child about patterns, look for these books in your local library.

- *One, Two, One Pair!* by Bruce McMillan (Scholastic, 1991)
- *Pattern* by Henry Pluckrose (Childrens Press, 1995)
- *Hide and Snake* by Keith Baker (Voyager/Harcourt Brace, 1991)

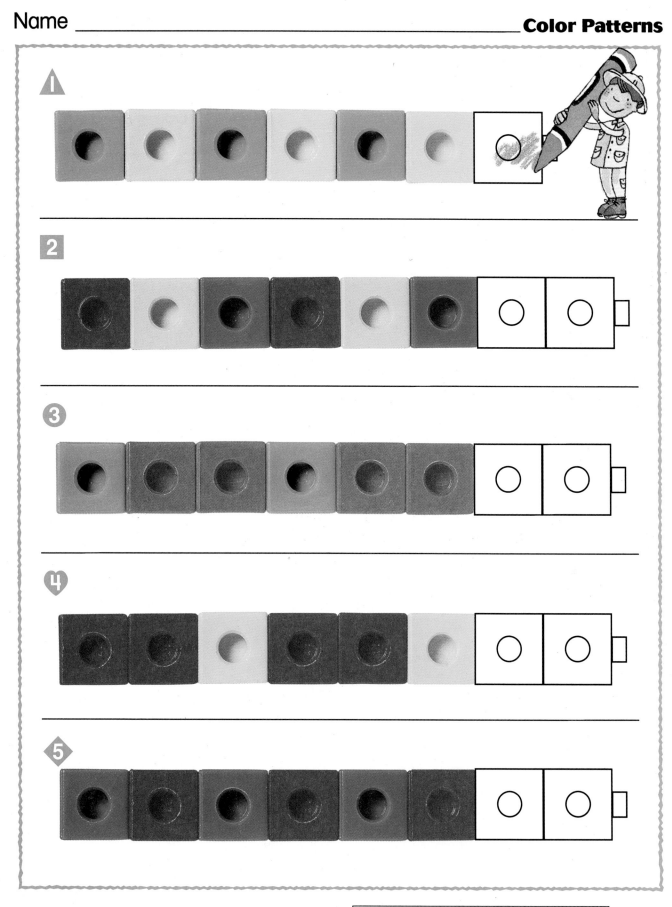

Directions Have children color snap cubes to continue each color pattern.

 Home Connection Collect small objects in two colors, such as blue and red buttons. Have your child create a repeating pattern with them.

B3

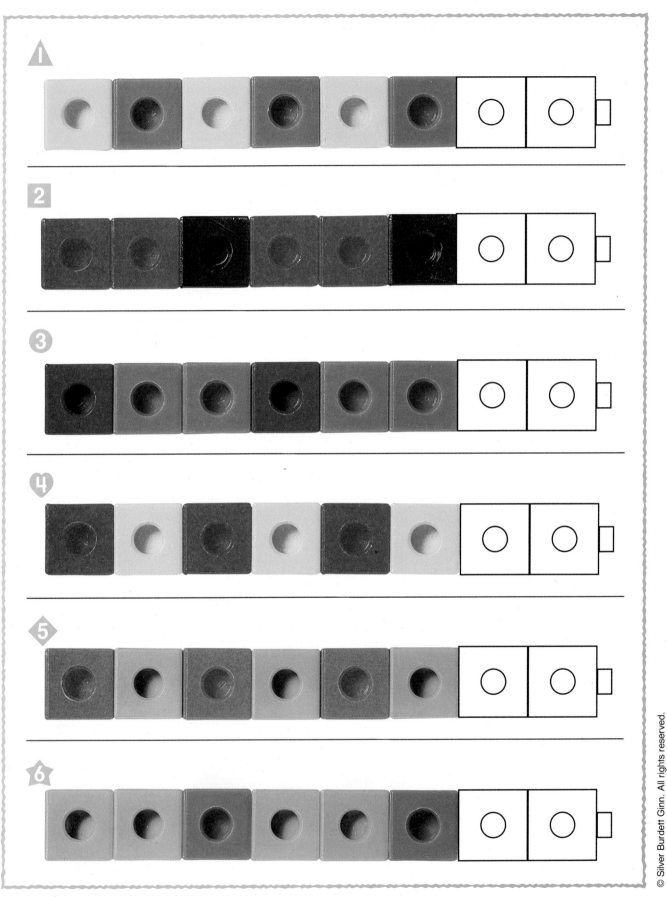

Directions Have children color the snap cubes to continue each
color pattern.

B4

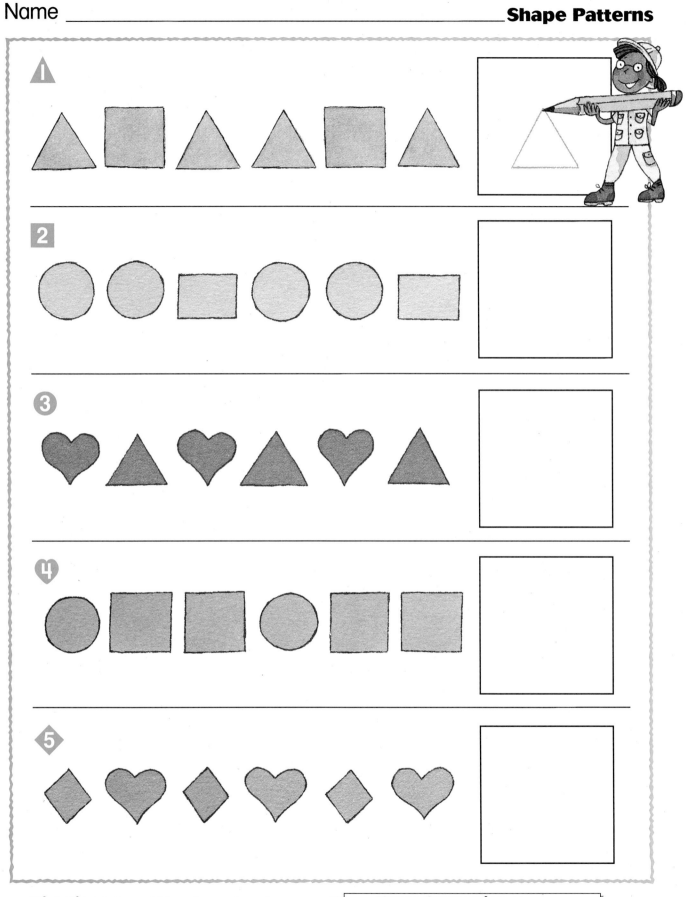

1

2

3

4

5

Directions Have children draw a shape to continue each shape pattern.

Home Connection Have your child use two different shapes of pasta to make a pattern necklace.

B5

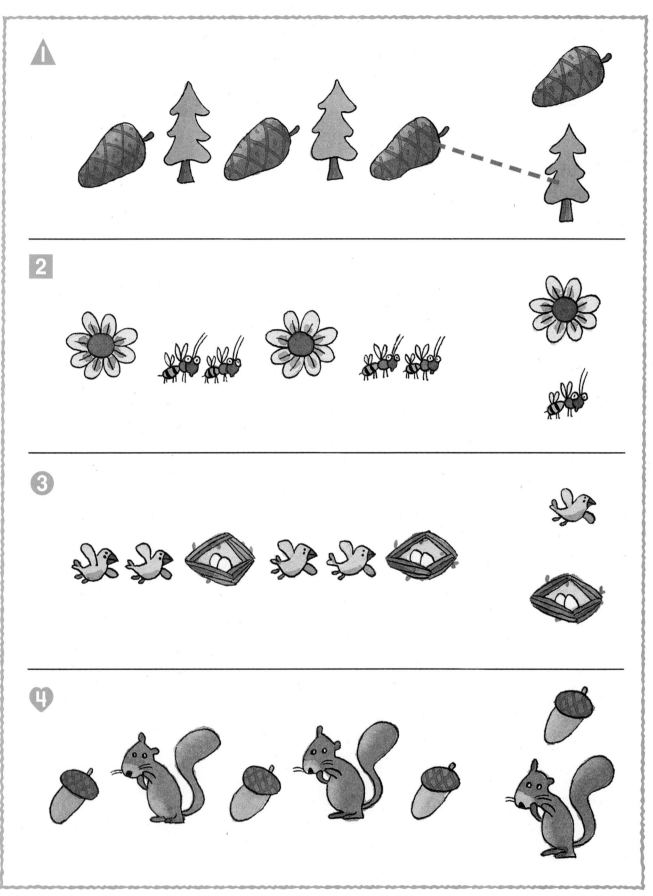

Directions Have children continue the shape pattern in each exercise by drawing a line to the picture that comes next.

B6

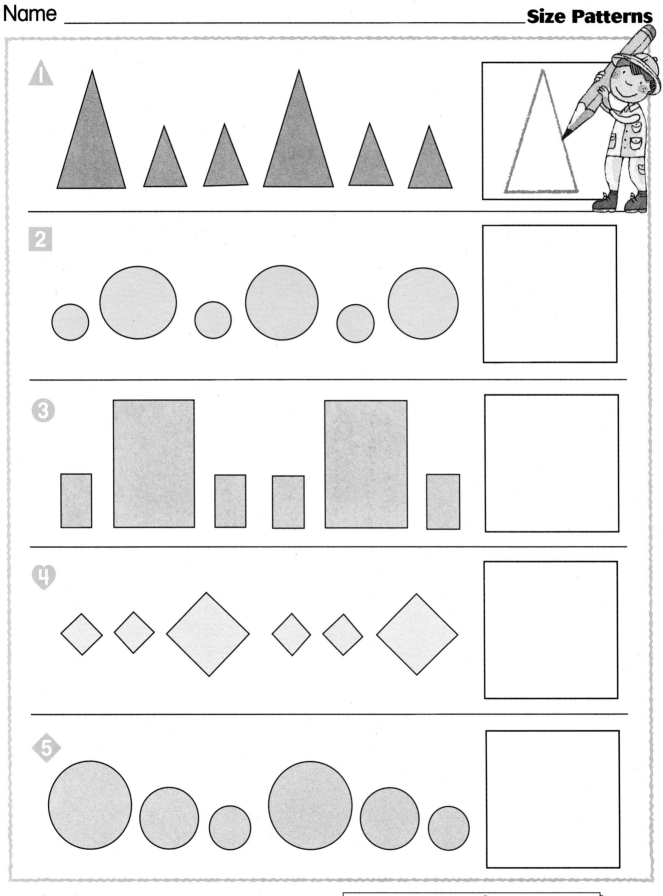

Directions Have children draw a shape to continue each size pattern.

Home Connection Gather some large and small white socks. Have your child create a size pattern.

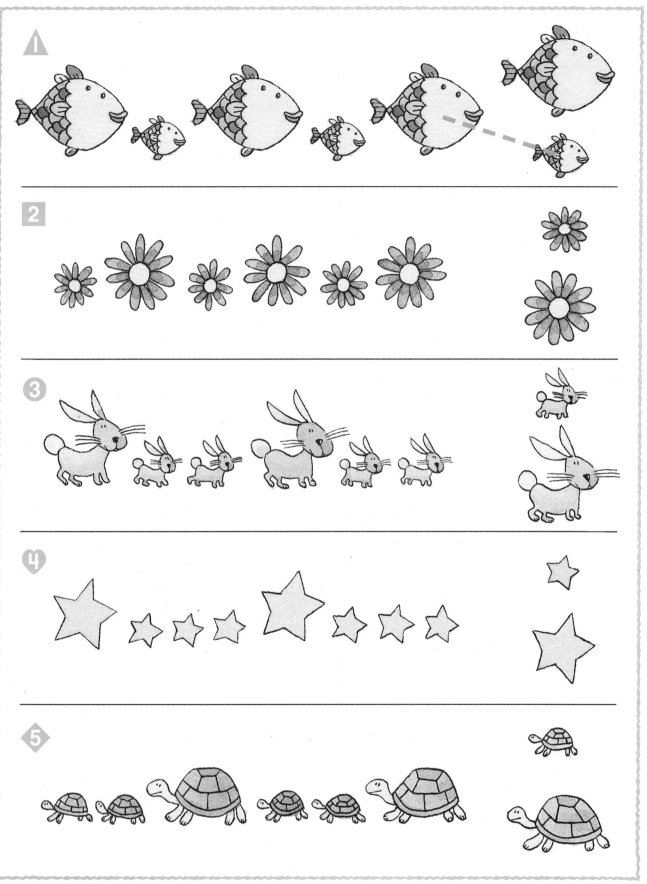

Directions Have children continue the size pattern in each exercise by drawing a line to the picture that comes next.

B8

INTERNET ACTIVITY
www.sbgmath.com

Problem-Solving
Guess and Check

STRATEGY
Understand
Plan
Solve
Look Back

Name _____

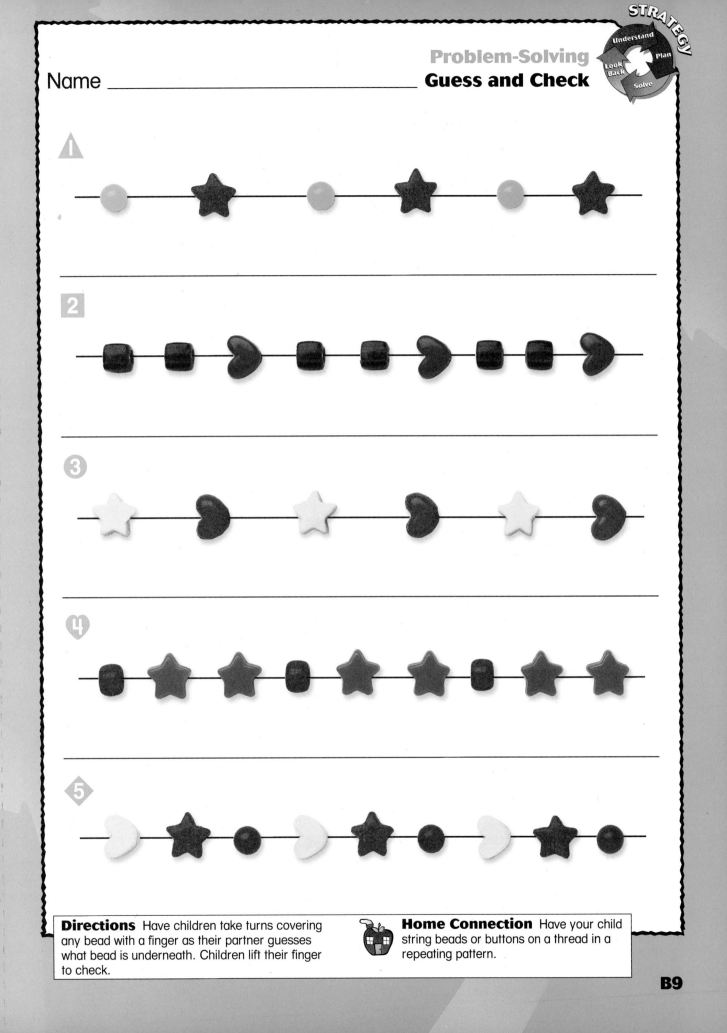

1

2

3

4

5

Directions Have children take turns covering any bead with a finger as their partner guesses what bead is underneath. Children lift their finger to check.

Home Connection Have your child string beads or buttons on a thread in a repeating pattern.

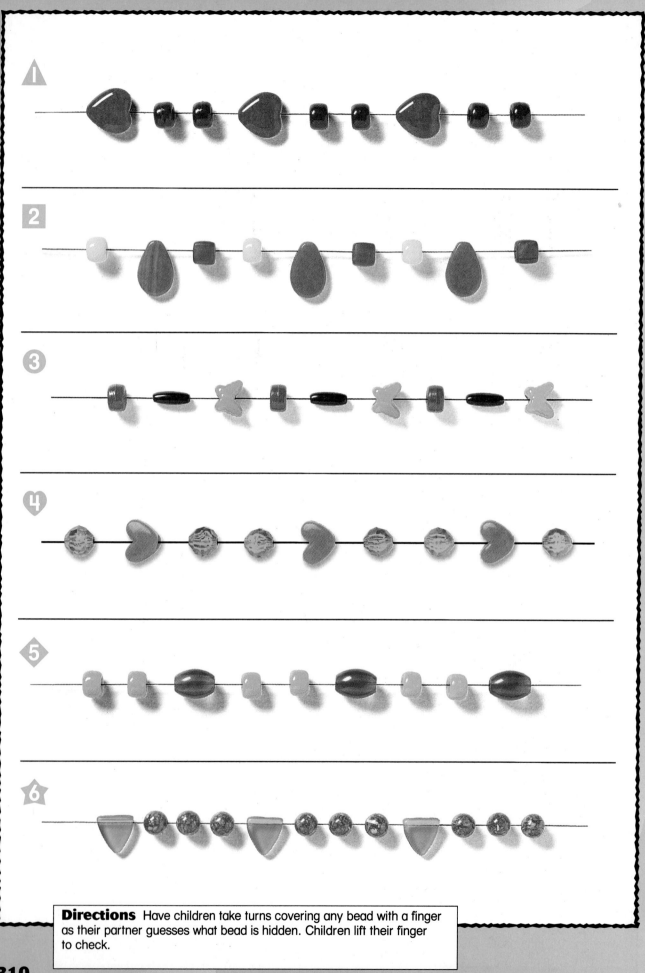

1

2

3

4

5

6

Directions Have children take turns covering any bead with a finger as their partner guesses what bead is hidden. Children lift their finger to check.

B10

Name _____ **Translating Patterns**

1.

2.

3.

4.

Directions Have children use cubes to act out each pattern. Have them color the cube shapes to show the same pattern with different colors.

Home Connection Have your child show one of the patterns above by using two different kinds of pasta.

B11

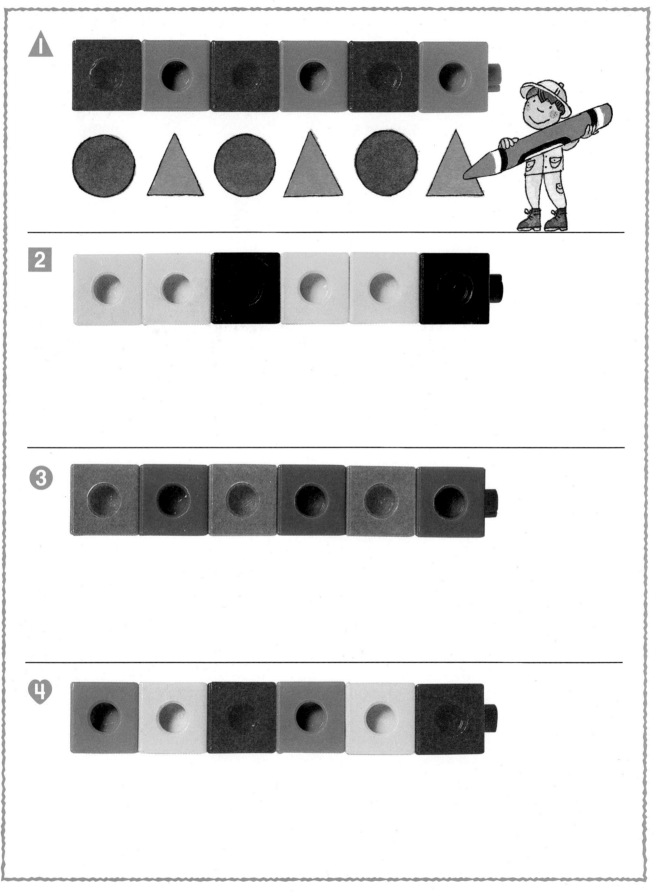

Directions Have children draw shapes or objects to show each pattern.

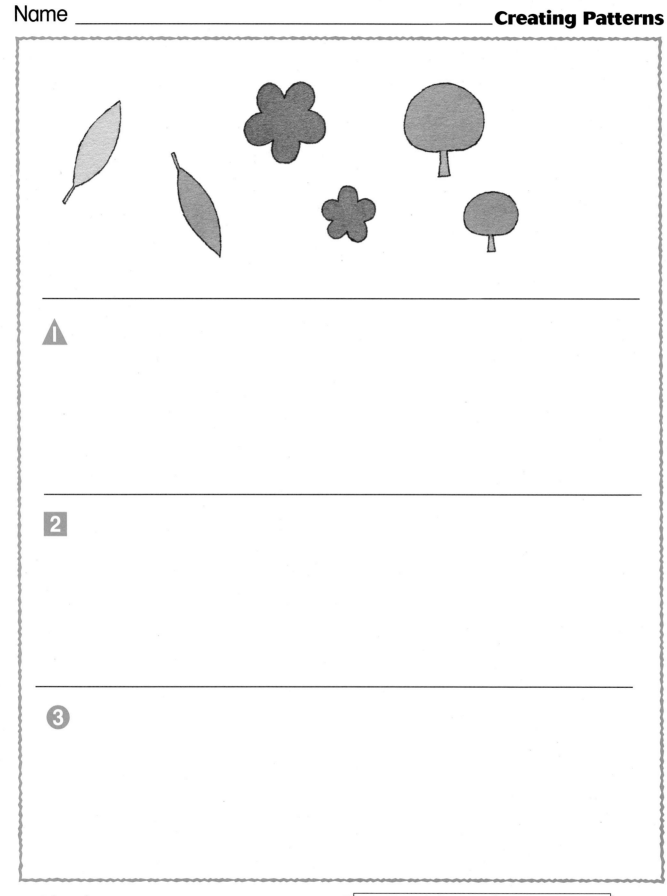

1

2

3

Directions Have children create various patterns, using the pictures at the top of the page. Then have them draw their patterns.

Home Connection Have your child create a pattern with buttons, cereal, dried beans, and other objects from home.

1

2

3

Directions Have children create various patterns, using the pictures at the top of the page. Then have them draw their patterns.

B14

Name _____ **Chapter Test**

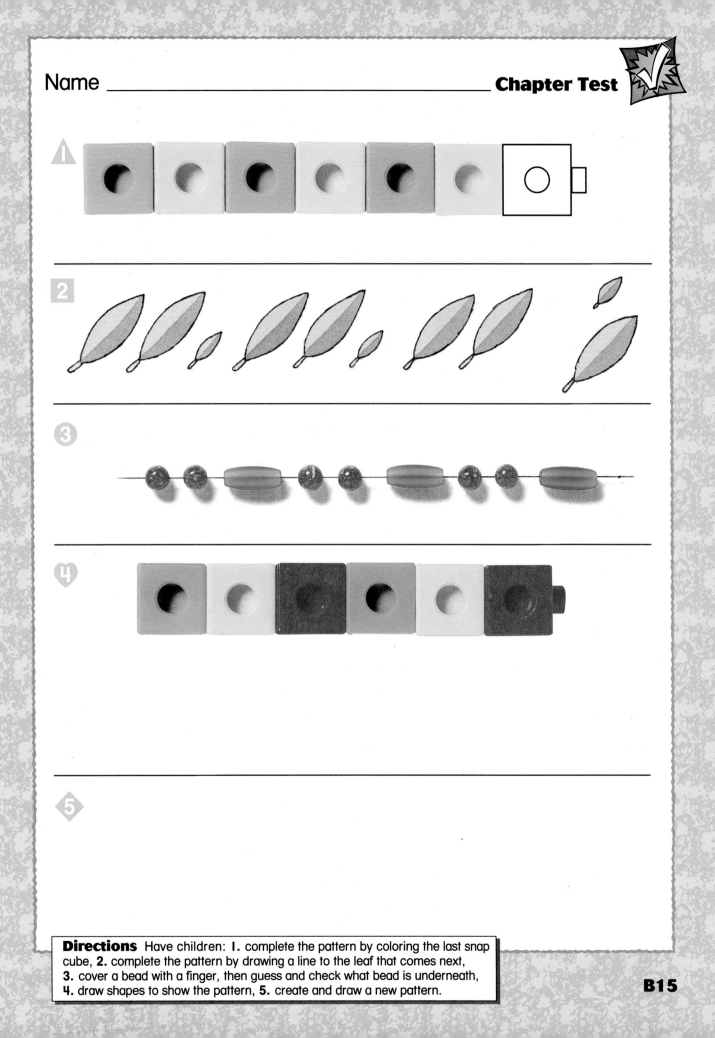

Directions Have children: **I.** complete the pattern by coloring the last snap cube, **2.** complete the pattern by drawing a line to the leaf that comes next, **3.** cover a bead with a finger, then guess and check what bead is underneath, **4.** draw shapes to show the pattern, **5.** create and draw a new pattern.

B15

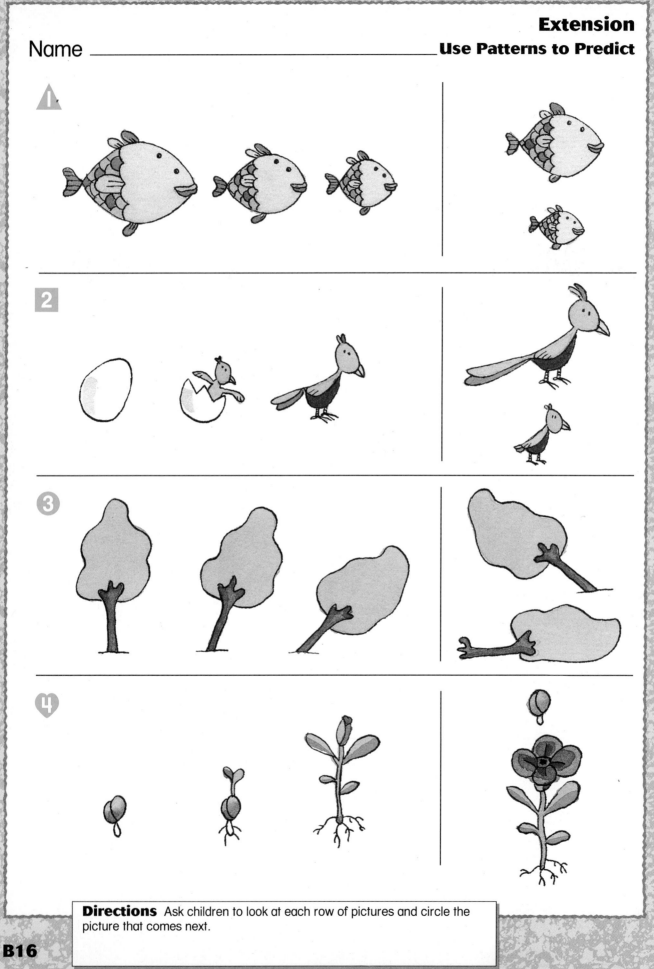

Name

⚠ 1

2

3

4

Directions Ask children to look at each row of pictures and circle the picture that comes next.

I'm a Friend

A Note to the Family

During the next few weeks, your child will be learning about numbers to 5. Here are some learning ideas you can share together.

At-Home Activities

- On your next trip to the store, invite your child to point out and name any numbers that he or she can find on signs, license plates, houses, and so on.

- The next time you are in a parking lot, ask your child how many blue (or any color) cars he or she can see. Encourage him or her to count aloud.

- Near the end of your next meal, ask your child to identify who has more of something (peas, for example) and who has fewer.

- Have your child plan and hold a party for his or her favorite toys. Encourage your child to use numbers, for example by counting place settings or gathering a specific number of food items. You might also ask him or her to line up five of the toys, then identify which is first, second, third, fourth, and fifth.

Read About It!

To read more with your child about numbers to 5, look for these books in your local library.

- *Dancing Feet* by Charlotte Agell (Harcourt Brace, 1994)
- *Five Little Monkeys Jumping on the Bed* by Eileen Christelow (Houghton Mifflin, 1994)
- *What Comes in 2s, 3s, & 4s?* by Suzanne Aker (Aladdin/Simon & Schuster, 1990)

Name _____ **More and Fewer**

1

2

3

4

Directions Tell children to draw a line from each marble in one group to a marble in the other group. Have them circle each group with more marbles.

Home Connection Have your child point out which groups on this page have fewer marbles and which groups on the back have more marbles.

C3

Directions Tell children to draw a line from each marble in one group to a marble in the other group. Have them circle each group with fewer marbles.

C4

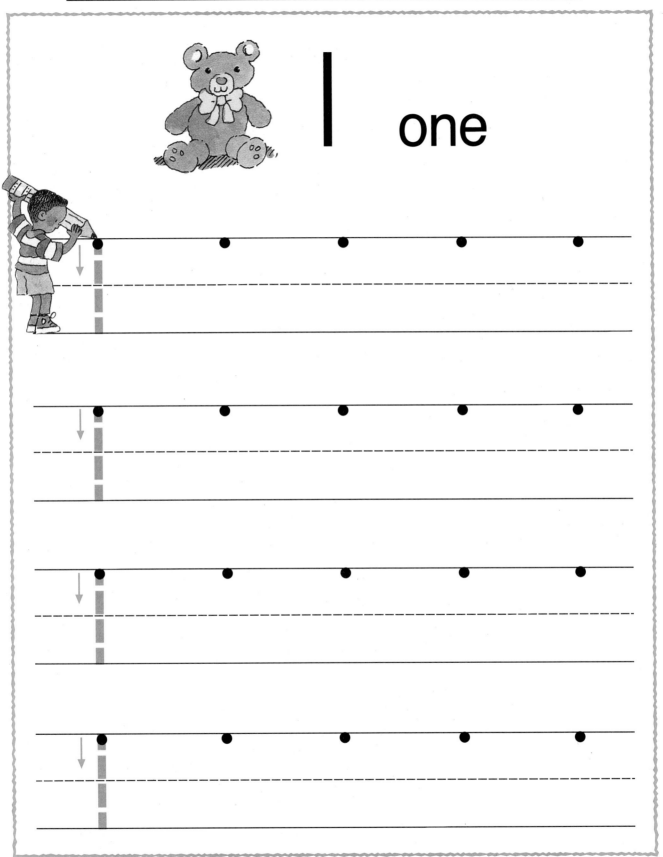

I one

Directions Have children practice writing the number 1, beginning each number at the black dot.

Home Connection Invite your child to find the numbers 1 and 2 around your home.

2 two

Directions Have children practice writing the number 2, beginning each number at the black dot.

3 three

Directions Have children practice writing the number 3, beginning each number at the black dot.

Home Connection Encourage your child to find the numbers 3 and 4 the next time you're at a store together.

C7

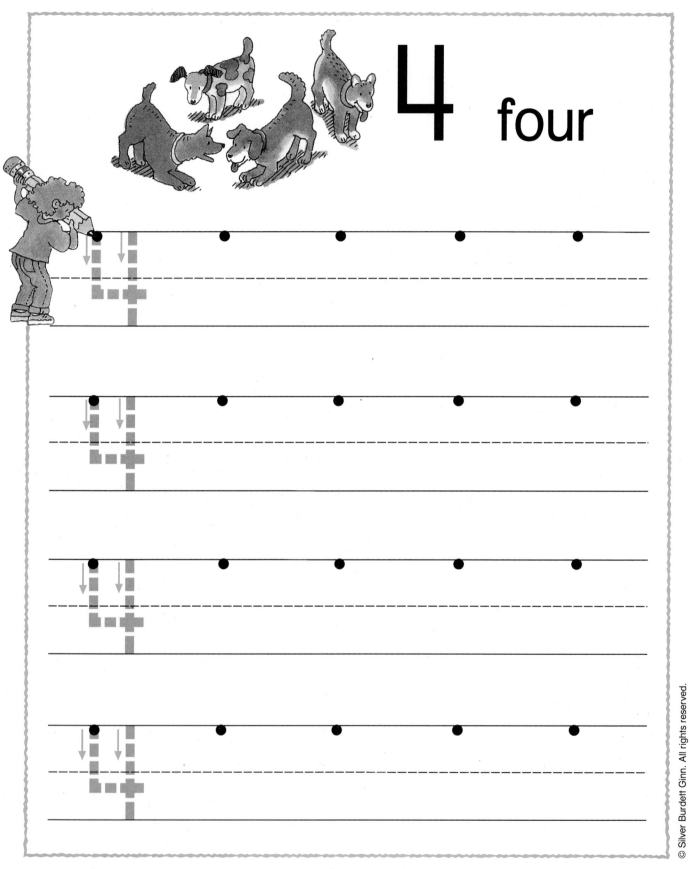

Directions Have children practice writing the number 4, beginning
each number at the black dot.

C8

5 five

Directions Have children practice writing the
number 5, beginning each number at the black dot.

 Home Connection On your next
walk or ride, invite your child to find the
numbers 5 and 0 on billboards and signs.

C9

0 zero

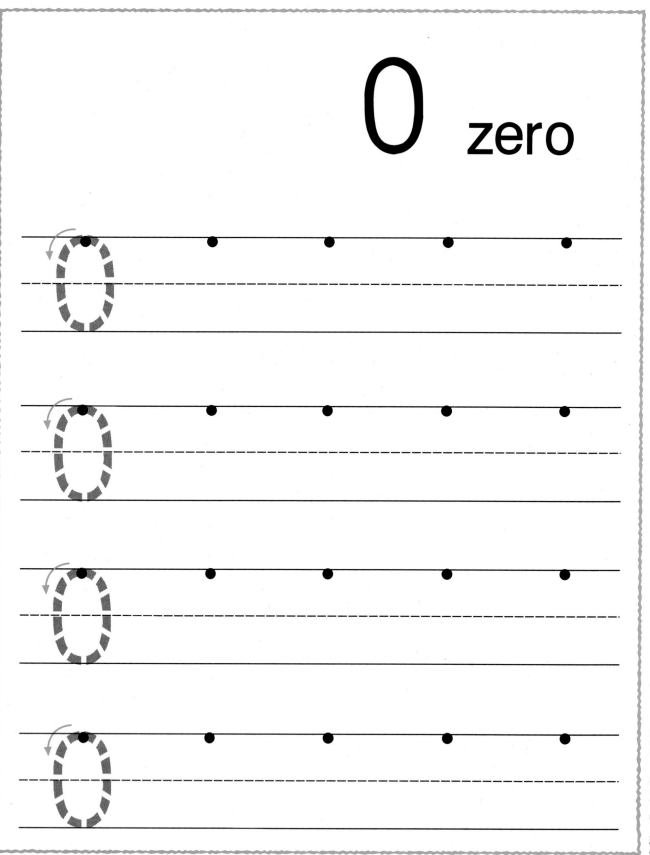

Directions Have children practice writing the number 0, beginning each number at the black dot.

C10

Directions Ask children to circle the first child in row 1, the second child in row 2, the third child in row 3, and the fourth child in row 4.

Home Connection Have your child use, first, second, third, fourth, and fifth to describe what he or she is doing when getting ready for bed.

Directions Ask children to circle the fourth child in row 1, the third child in row 2, the fifth child in row 3, the first child in row 4, and the second child in row 5.

INTERNET ACTIVITY
www.sbgmath.com

Name _____

Sorting by Color

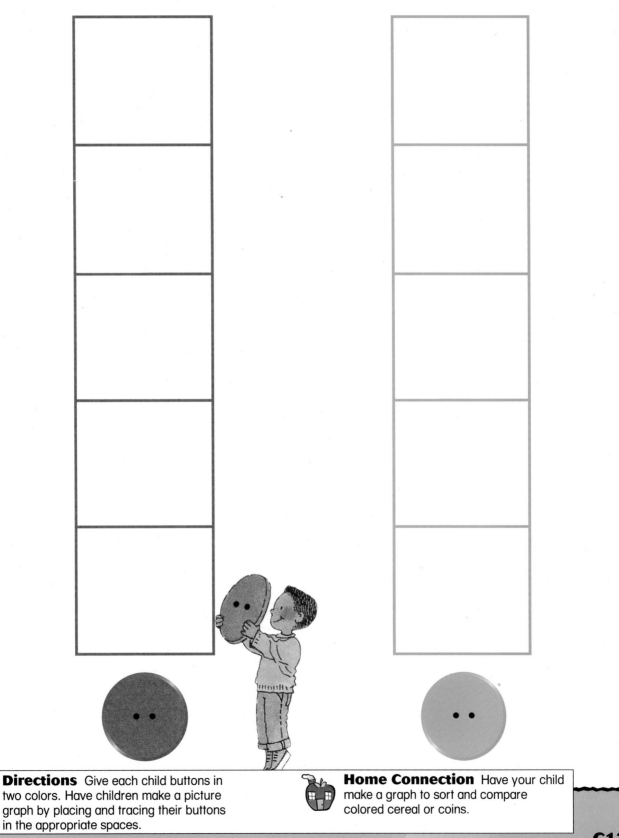

Directions Give each child buttons in two colors. Have children make a picture graph by placing and tracing their buttons in the appropriate spaces.

Home Connection Have your child make a graph to sort and compare colored cereal or coins.

Sorting Objects

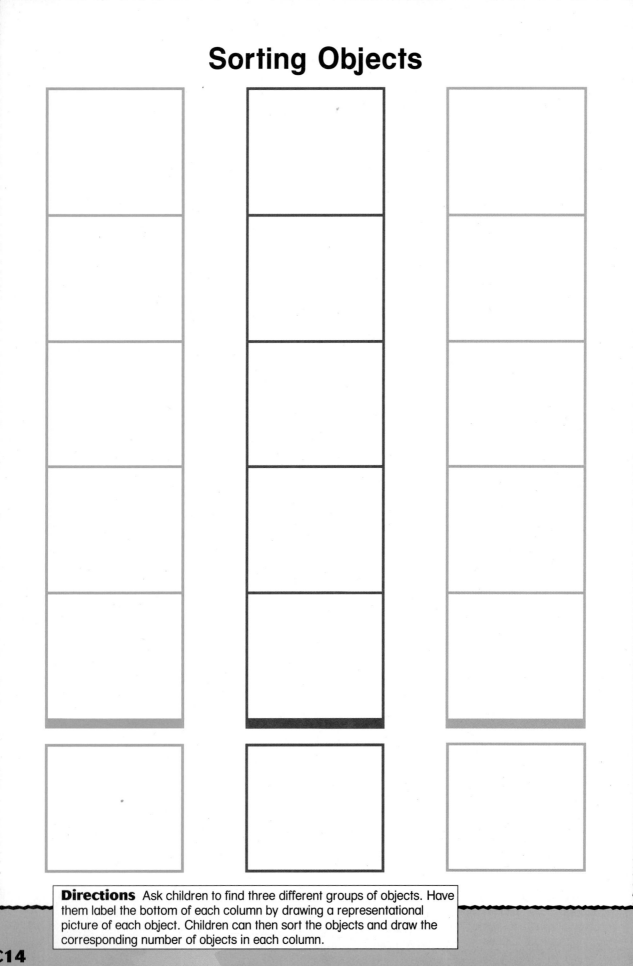

Directions Ask children to find three different groups of objects. Have them label the bottom of each column by drawing a representational picture of each object. Children can then sort the objects and draw the corresponding number of objects in each column.

C14

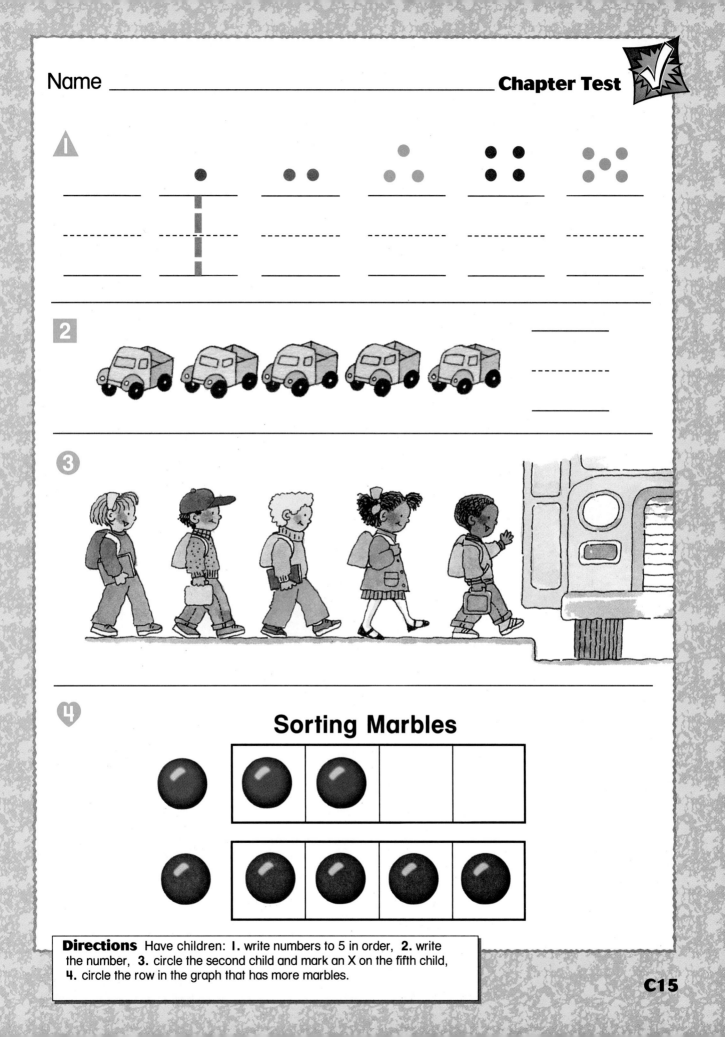

Sorting Marbles

Directions Have children: **1.** write numbers to 5 in order, **2.** write the number, **3.** circle the second child and mark an X on the fifth child, **4.** circle the row in the graph that has more marbles.

C15

Name _____

0	1	2	3	4
5	0	1	2	3

Directions Have children write the numbers 0 to 5 in order over and over to fill the chart. Then have them color all the boxes that have the number 5, using the same color each time. Ask them to identify the pattern.

C16

I'm an Artist

A Note to the Family

**During the next few weeks, your
child will be learning about shapes.
Here are some learning ideas you
can share together.**

At-Home Activities

• Encourage your child to find shapes around your home—dishes for
circles, books for rectangles, and so on.

• On your next road trip, ask your child to find objects that have a
particular shape. For example, *Can you see anything that is shaped
like a triangle?* You could also point out an object, such as a road
sign, and ask your child to name its shape.

• With markers, crayons, or paints, have your child create a picture
using as many rectangles (or any shape) as he or she can.

• The next time you have pancakes, cut one into three unequal pieces,
such as one large and two small pieces. Ask your child if the pieces
are equal.

• Have your child use a butter knife to practice cutting a slice of bread
into equal parts, such as halves and quarters.

Read About It!

To read more about shapes with your child, look for these books in
your local library.

• *A Fishy Shape Story* by Joanne and David Wylie (Childrens
Press, 1984)

• *Shape Space* by Cathryn Falwell (Clarion, 1992)

• *Eating Fractions* by Bruce McMillan (Scholastic, 1993)

Directions Have children color all the squares in the picture.

 Home Connection Ask your child to find squares and circles around your home.

D3

Directions Have children color all the circles in the picture.

D4

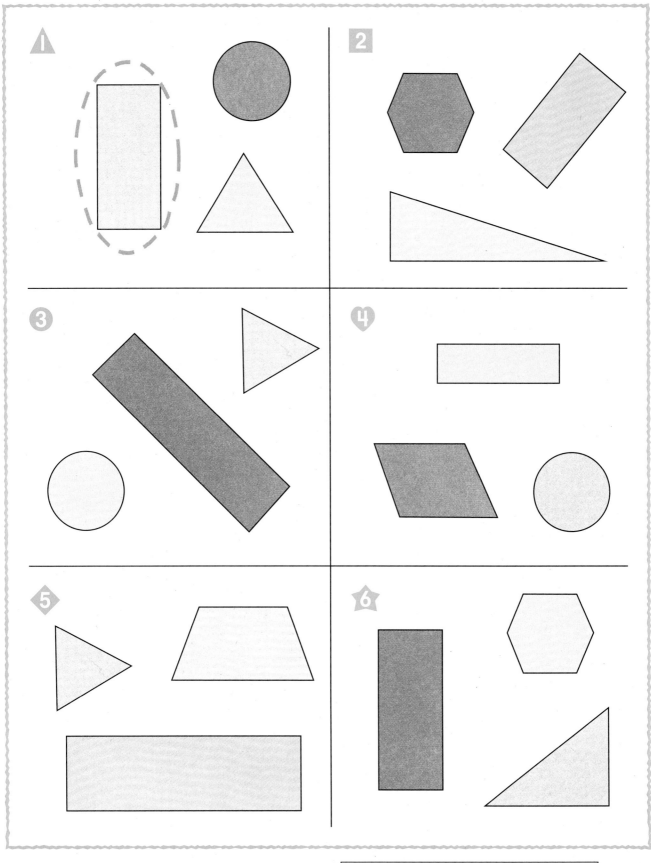

Directions Ask children to circle each rectangle.

Home Connection On your next car or bus ride, challenge your child to find rectangles and triangles.

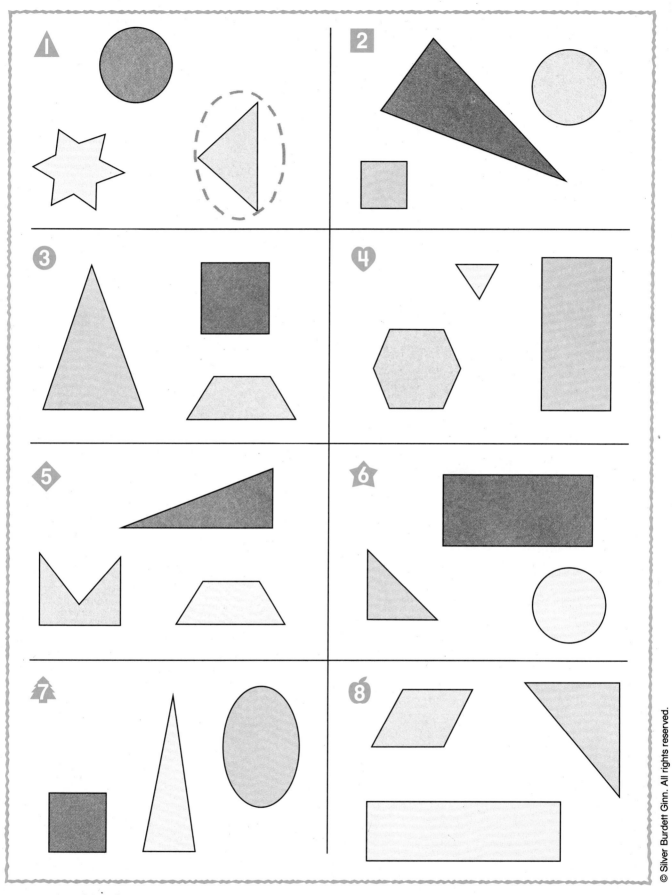

Directions Have children circle each triangle.

D6

Name _____ **Exploring Equal Parts**

1

2

3

4

Directions Ask children to circle each item that is cut into equal parts.

Home Connection Cut one bread slice into two equal parts and another into two unequal parts. Have your child identify the one cut into equal parts.

D7

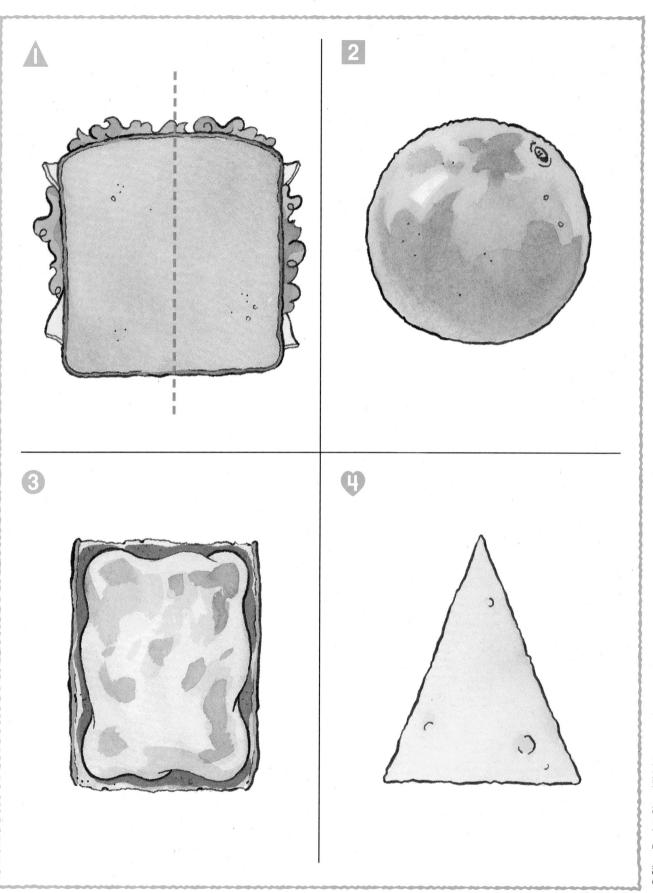

Directions Have children draw a line through each item to make two parts or halves that are about equal.

D8

Problem-Solving
Act It Out

STRATEGY
Understand
Plan
Look Back
Solve

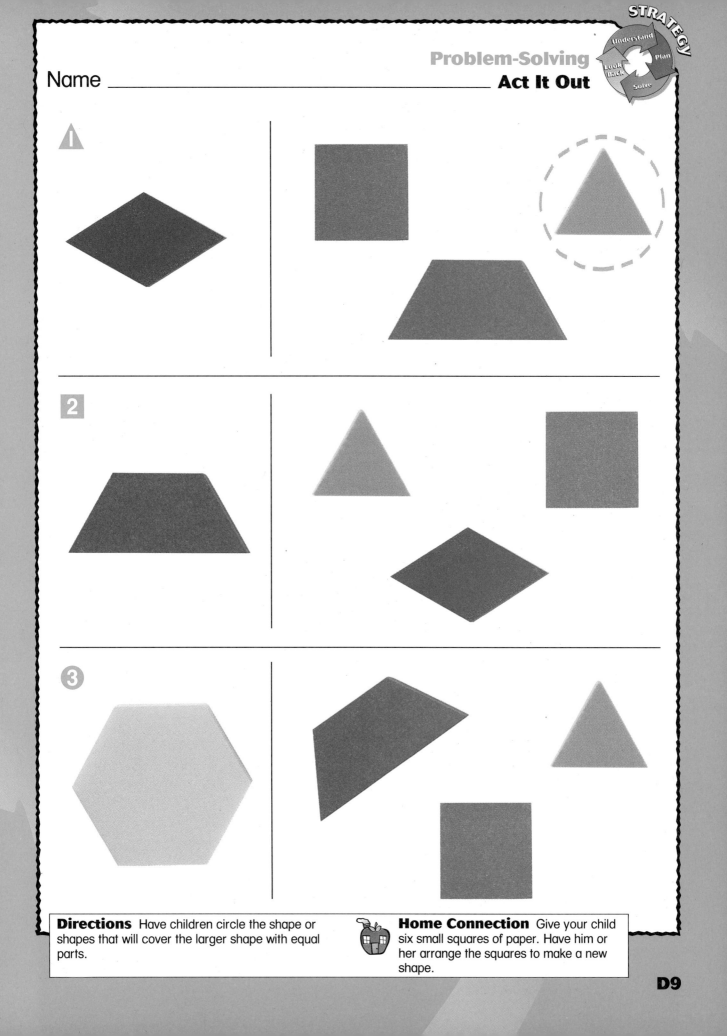

1

2

3

Directions Have children circle the shape or shapes that will cover the larger shape with equal parts.

Home Connection Give your child six small squares of paper. Have him or her arrange the squares to make a new shape.

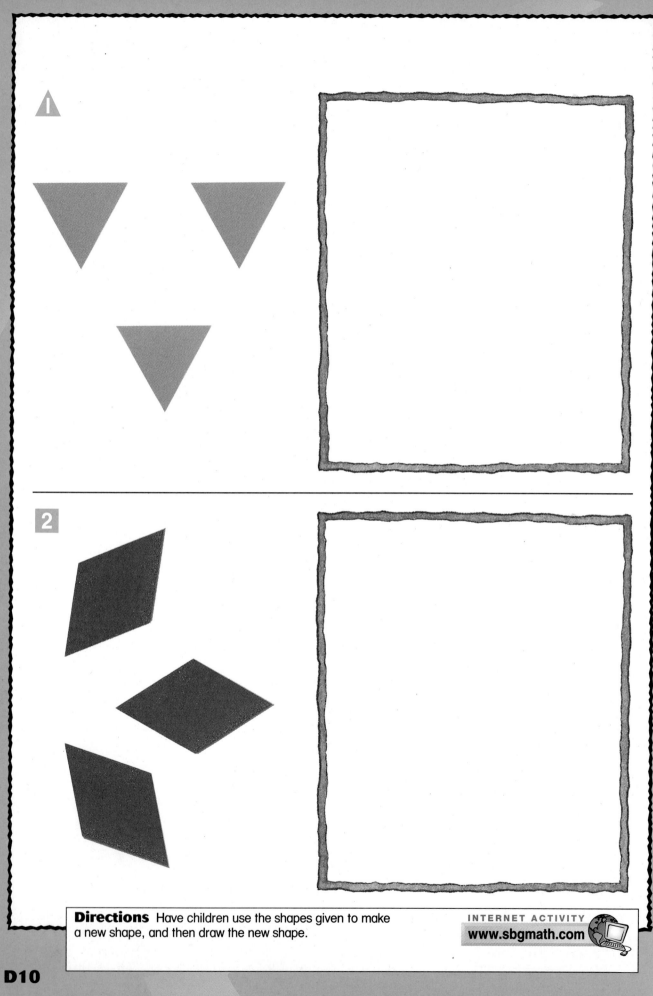

Directions Have children use the shapes given to make a new shape, and then draw the new shape.

INTERNET ACTIVITY
www.sbgmath.com

Name _____

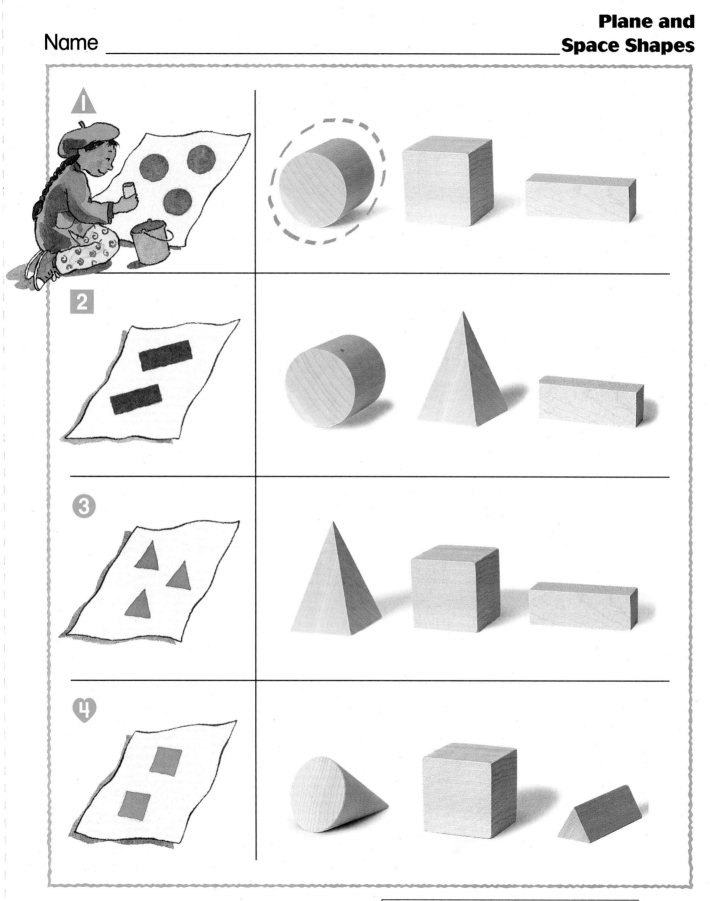

Directions Have children circle the kind of block that could make each shape print.

Home Connection Challenge your child to find objects around your home that could make circle or square shapes.

D11

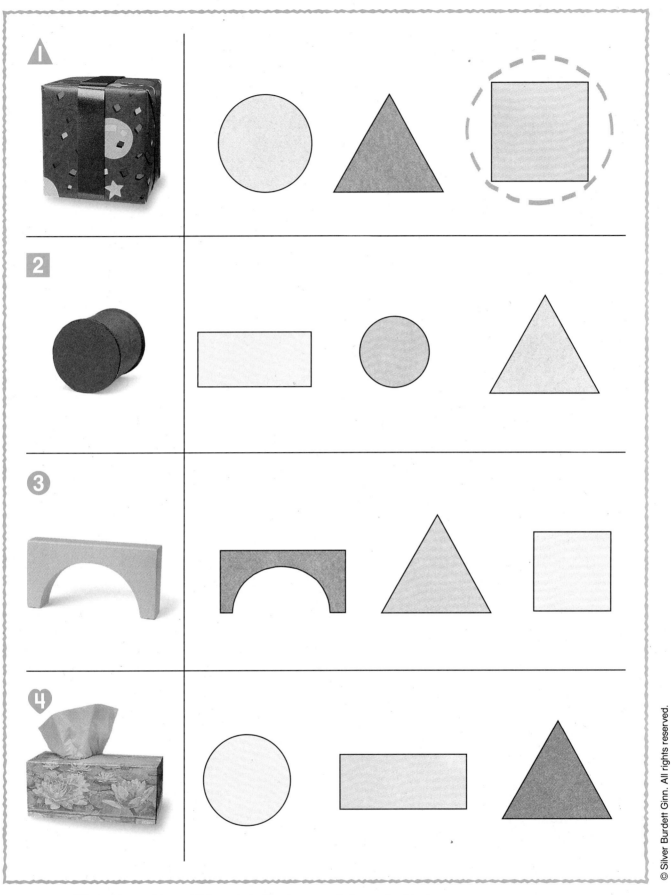

Directions Have children circle the shape made by each object.

D12

Shapes

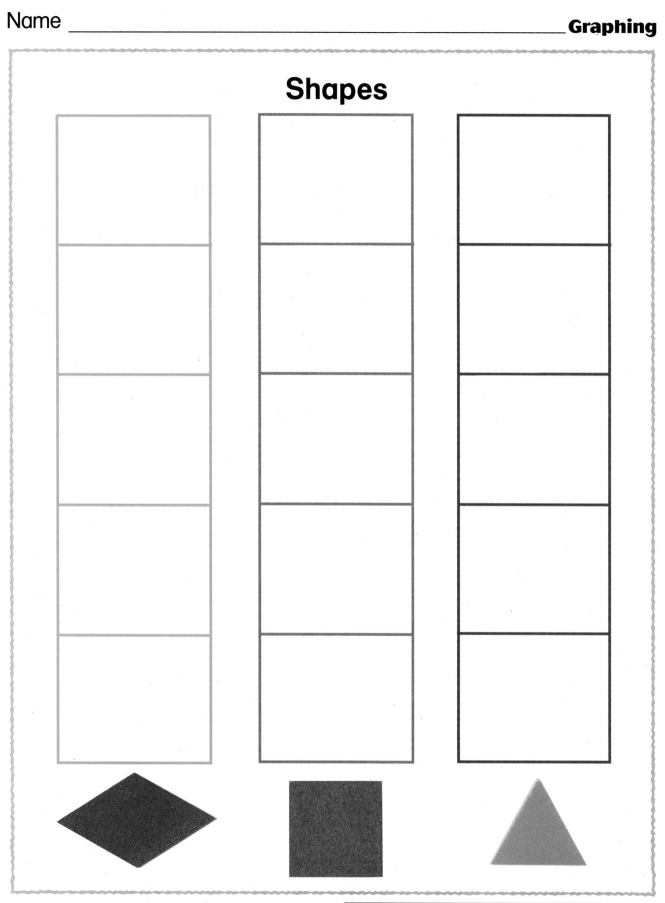

Directions Have children sort pattern blocks to make a real graph. Then have them draw the shapes in the appropriate columns.

Home Connection With your child, look for shapes in your home. Count and graph the shapes you find.

D13

Our Favorite Shapes

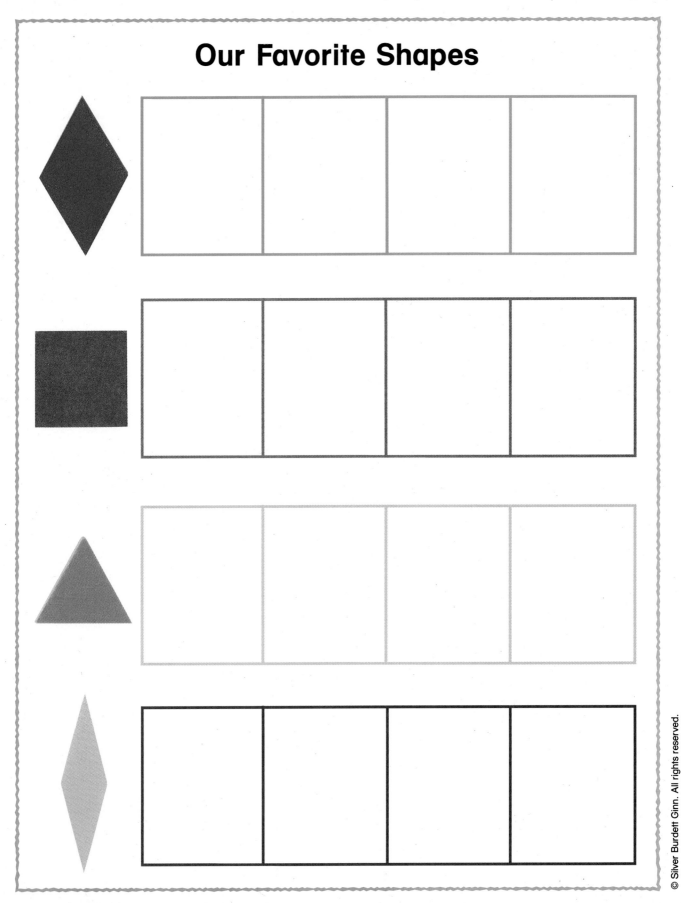

Directions Have each group member name his or her favorite
shape. Have each child draw those shapes in the appropriate columns.

D14

Name _____ **Chapter Test**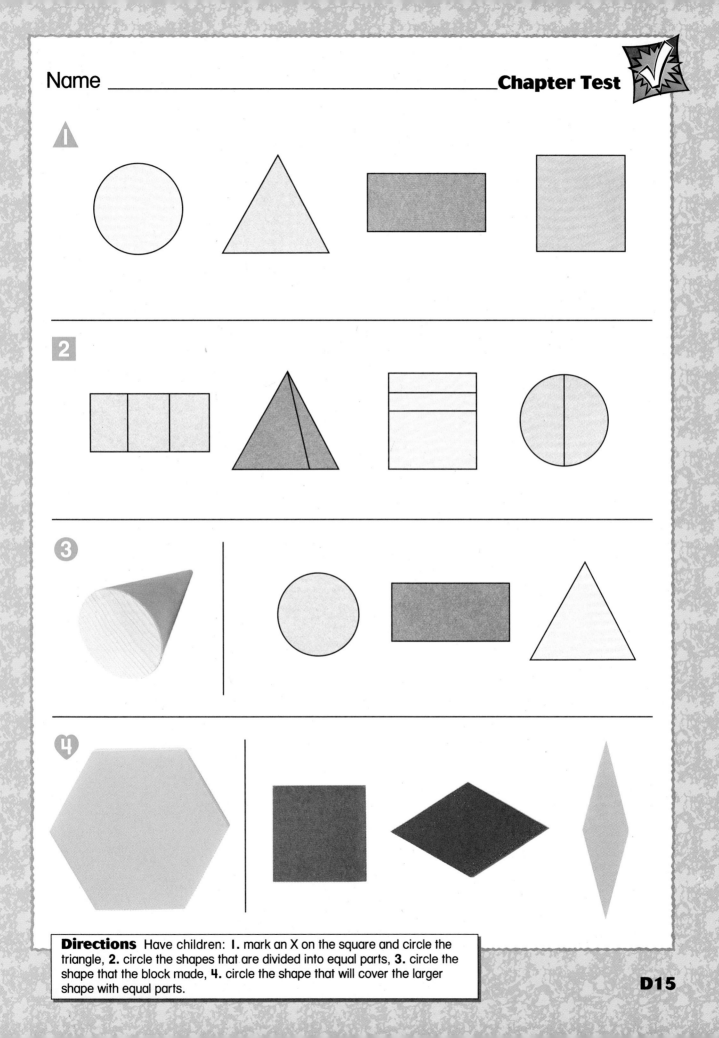

Directions Have children: **1.** mark an X on the square and circle the triangle, **2.** circle the shapes that are divided into equal parts, **3.** circle the shape that the block made, **4.** circle the shape that will cover the larger shape with equal parts.

D15

Name _____

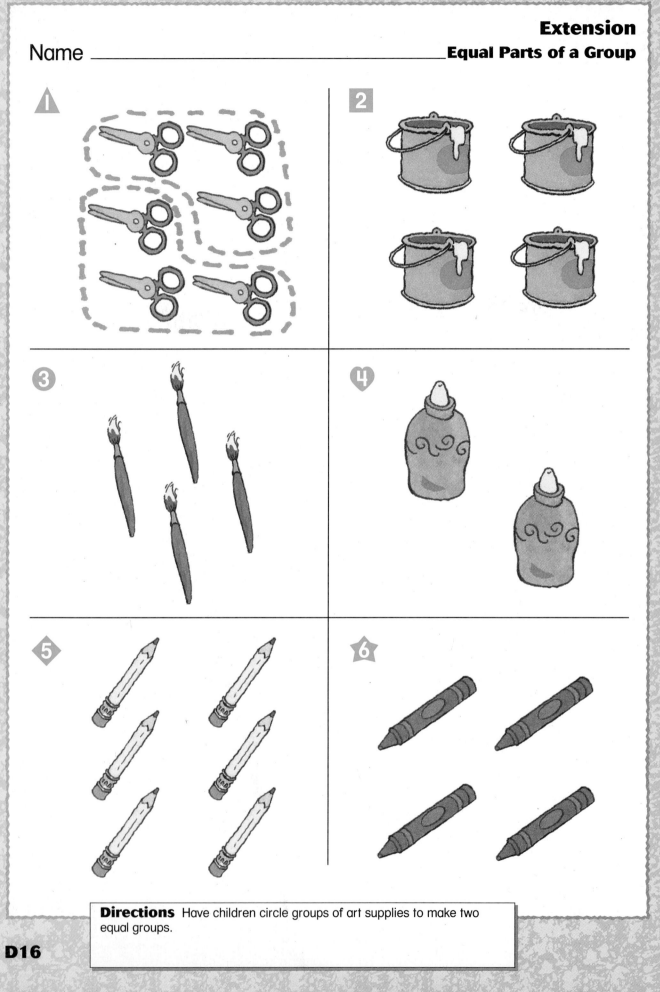

Directions Have children circle groups of art supplies to make two equal groups.

A Note to the Family

During the next few weeks, your child will be learning numbers to 10. Here are some learning ideas you can share together.

At-Home Activities

- When going up and down stairs, encourage your child to count forward from 0 to 10 then backward from 10 to 0.

- Write all of the numbers from 0 to 10 on a piece of paper, then cut them apart to make cards. Have your child put the number cards in order from 0 to 10.

- Line up ten animal crackers in a row, all facing in the same direction. Point out the first cracker, then ask your child to identify the *sixth* cracker. Continue for *seventh, eighth, ninth*, and *tenth*.

- Display seven dried beans (or another food item) and have your child count them. Write the number seven on a paper cup and turn it upside down to cover the beans. Put two more beans next to the cup and ask your child to tell how many beans there are in all. Encourage him or her to begin counting at seven (seven . . . eight, nine).

Read About It!

To read more with your child about numbers to 10, look for these books in your local library.

- *Emeka's Gift* by Ifeoma Onyefulu (Cobblehill, 1995)
- *Feast for 10* by Cathryn Falwell (Clarion, 1993)
- *Ten Flashing Fireflies* by Philemon Sturges (North-South, 1995)

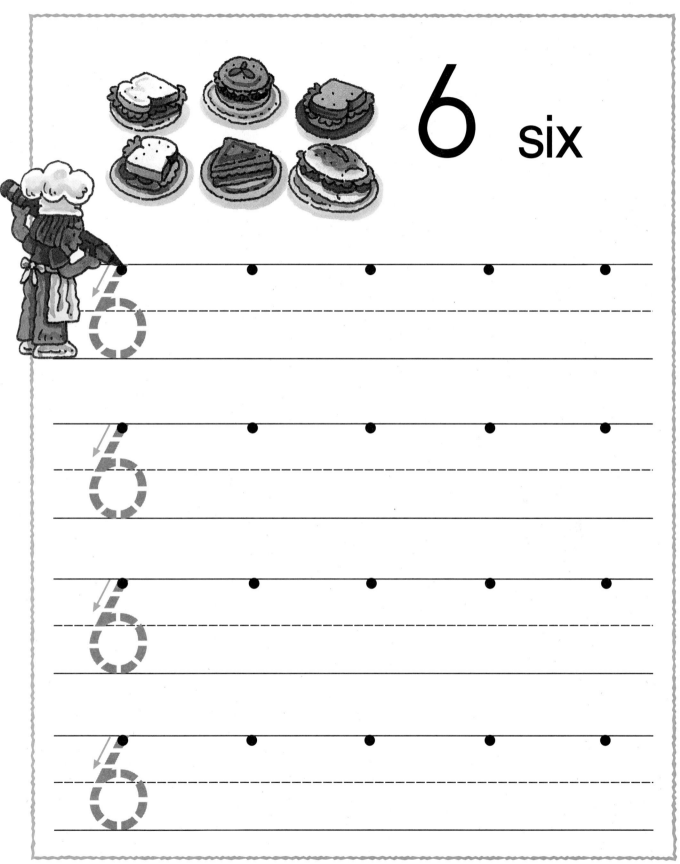

6 six

Directions Have children practice writing the number 6, beginning each number at the black dot.

Home Connection Ask your child to find the numbers 6 and 7 around your home.

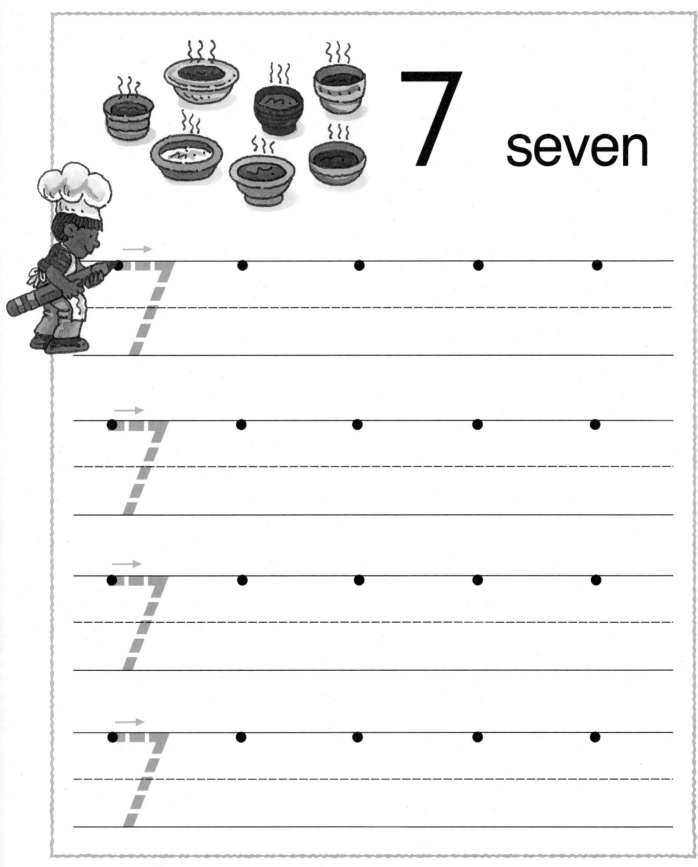

7 seven

Directions Have children practice writing the number 7, beginning each number at the black dot.

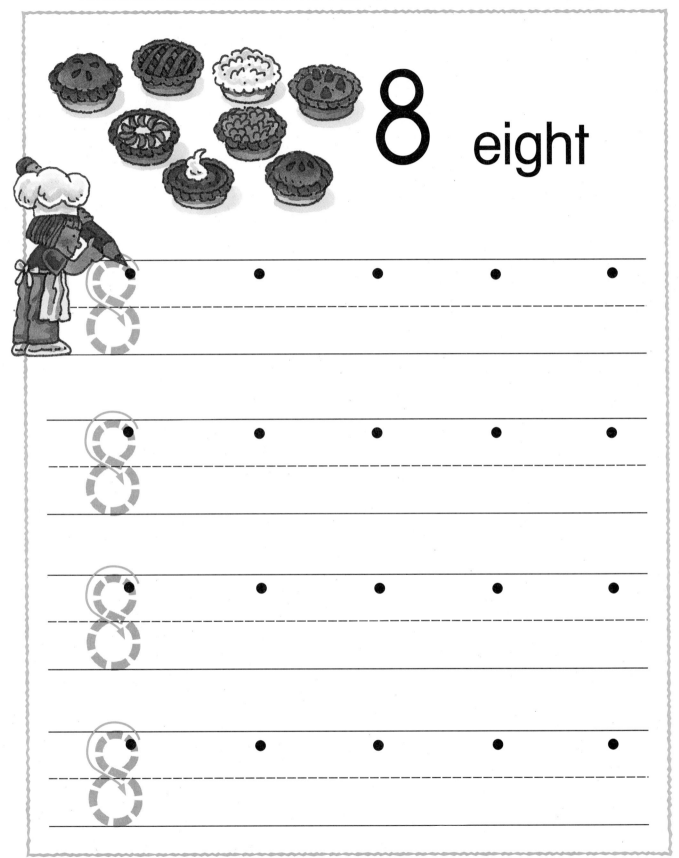

8 eight

Directions Have children practice writing the number 8, beginning each number at the black dot.

Home Connection The next time you're at a store, ask your child to point out the numbers 8, 9, and 10 on labels or signs.

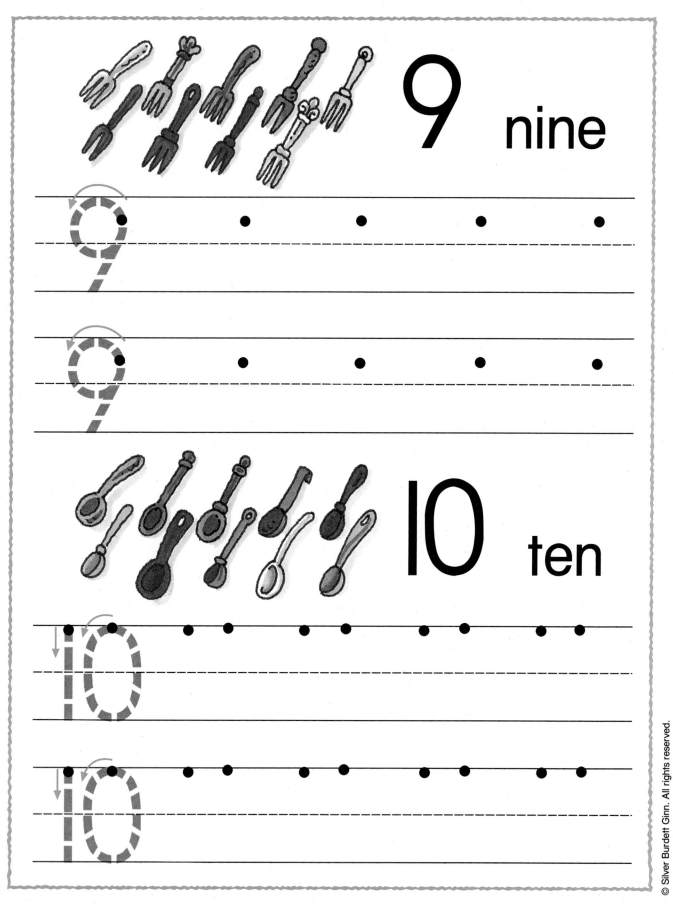

9 nine

10 ten

Directions Have children practice writing the numbers 9 and 10, beginning each number at the black dot.

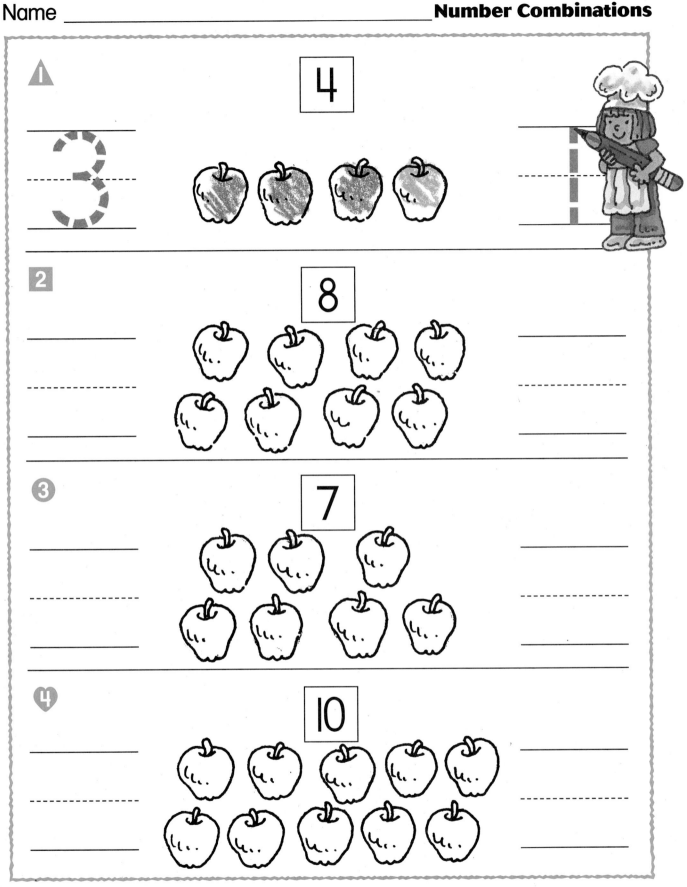

1 3 4

2 8

3 7

4 10

Directions In each exercise, have children color some apples red and the rest green. Then have them write how many of each color.

Home Connection Collect six crayons of two different colors. Have your child count the crayons and then count how many there are of each color.

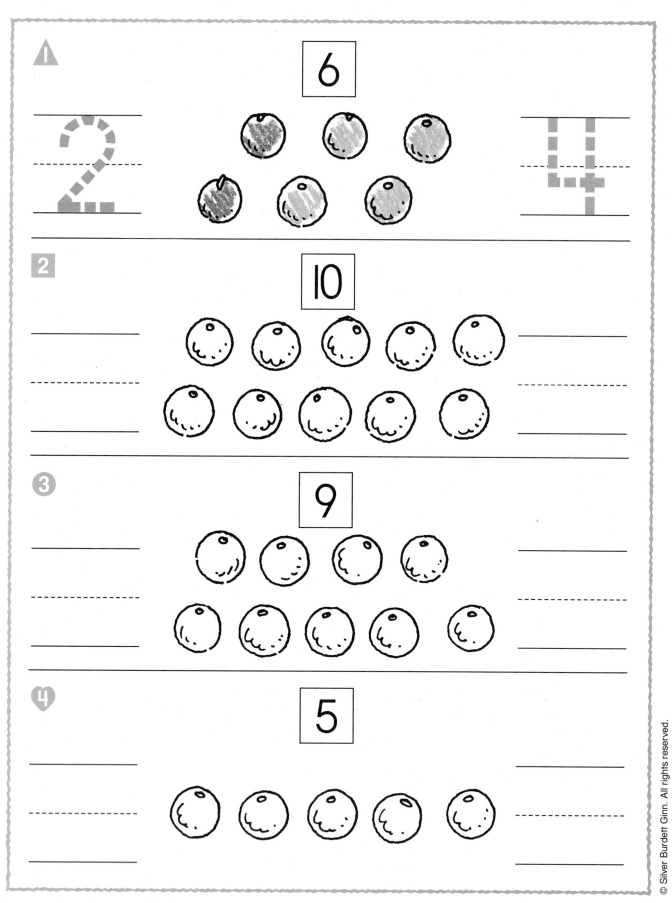

Directions In each exercise, have children color some grapes purple and the rest green. Then have them write how many of each color.

E8

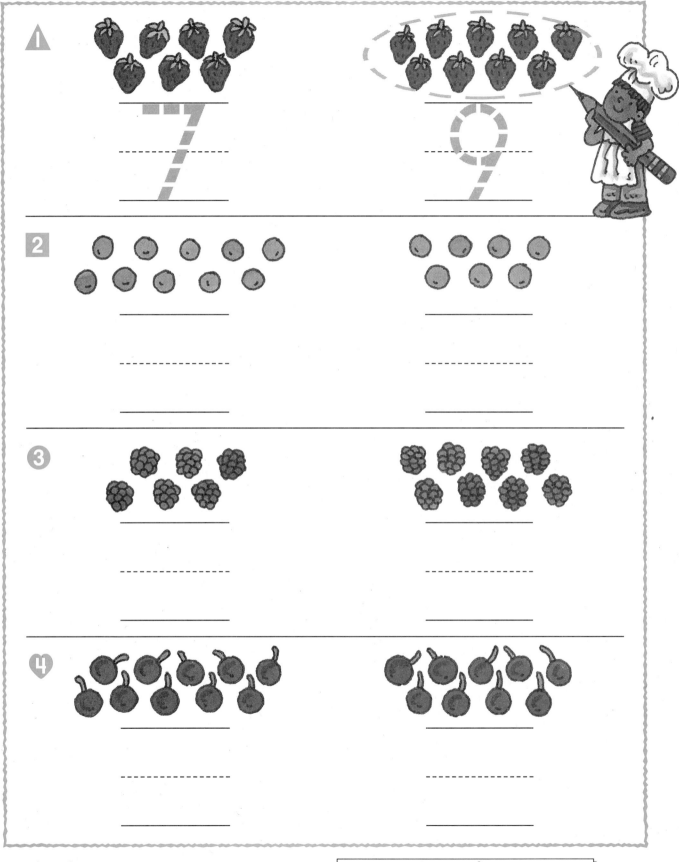

1. 7   9

2.

3.

4.

Directions Have children count each group of fruit and write the number. Ask them to circle the group with more pieces of fruit.

Home Connection Make two small groups of food, such as six peanuts and eight peanuts. Ask your child, "Which group has more peanuts?"

E9

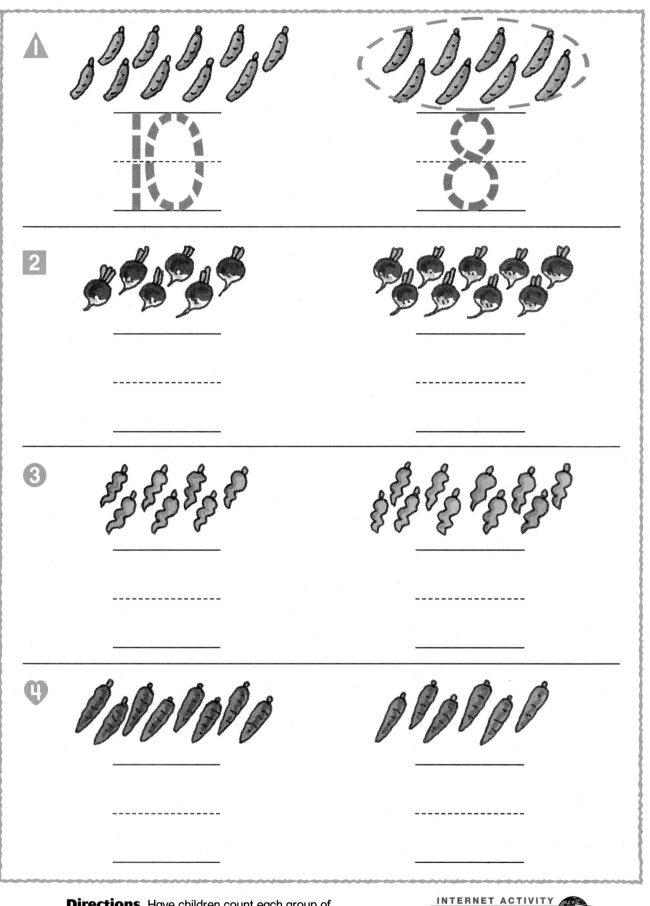

Directions Have children count each group of vegetables and write the number. Ask them to circle the group with fewer vegetables.

E10

INTERNET ACTIVITY
www.sbgmath.com

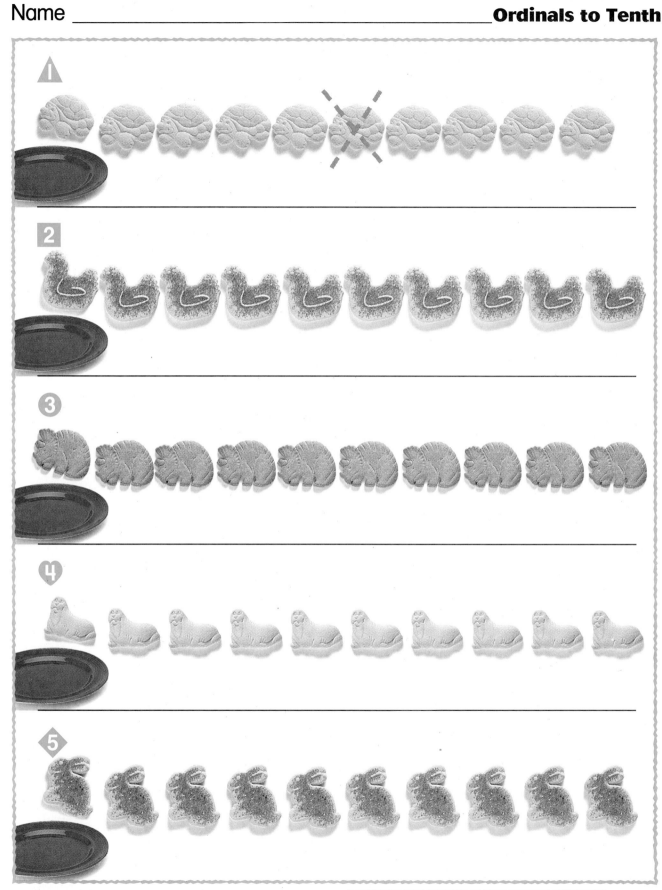

Directions Ask children to mark an X on the sixth cookie in row 1, the seventh cookie in row 2, the eighth cookie in row 3, the ninth cookie in row 4, and the tenth cookie in row 5.

Home Connection Take a walk with your child. Ask your child to identify the sixth floor of a building or sixth house on the street.

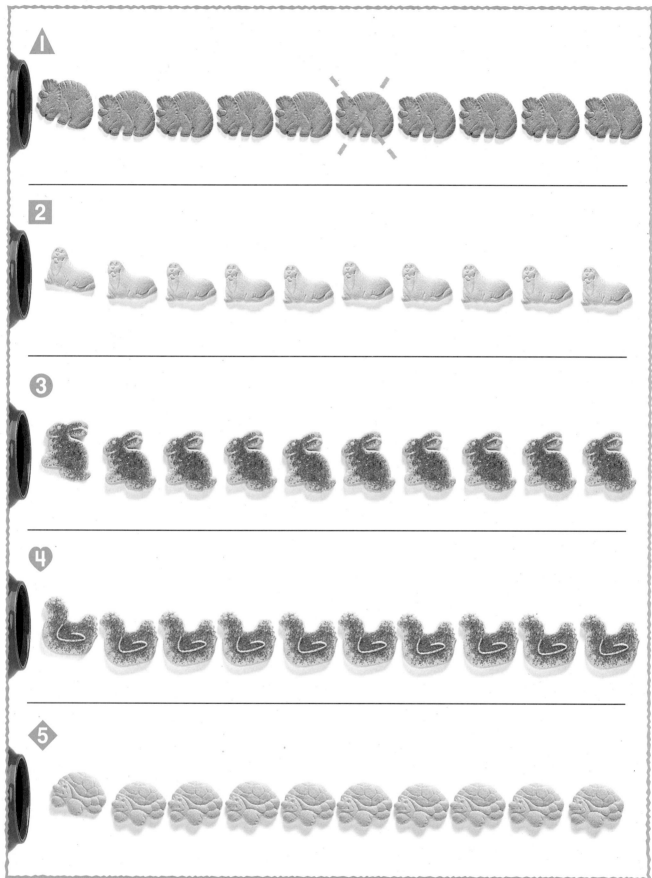

Directions Ask children to mark an X on the sixth cookie in row 1, the seventh cookie in row 2, the eighth cookie in row 3, the ninth cookie in row 4, and the tenth cookie in row 5.

E12

STRATEGY

Understand
Plan
Look Back
Solve

Problem-Solving
Make a Table

Name _____

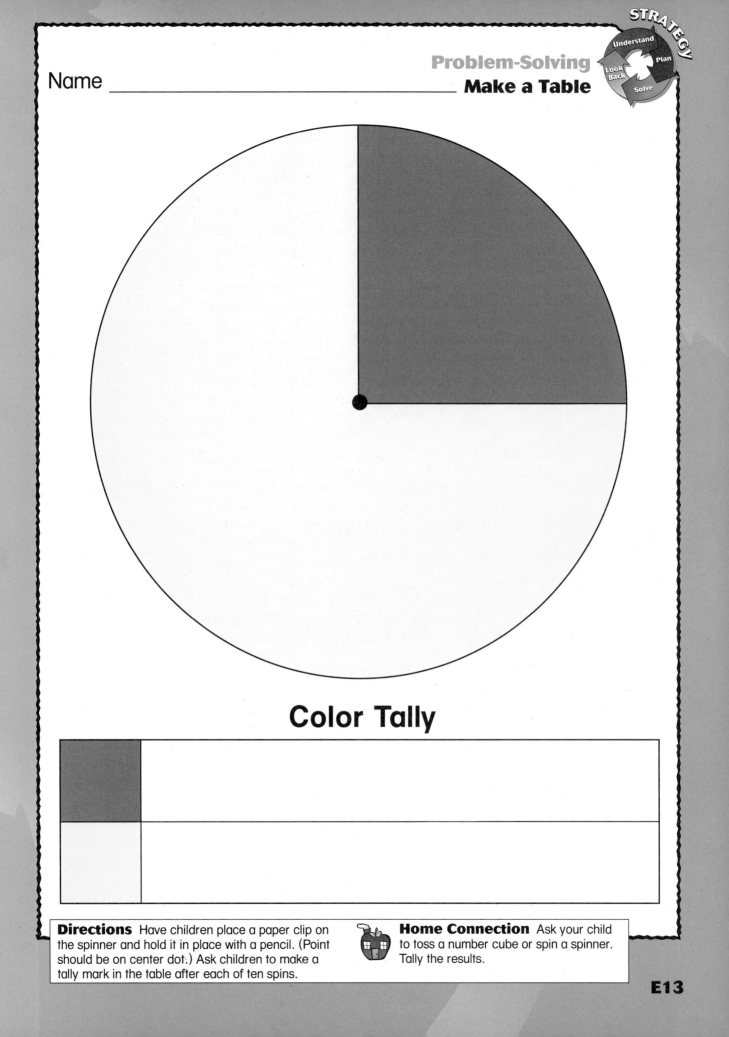

Color Tally

Directions Have children place a paper clip on the spinner and hold it in place with a pencil. (Point should be on center dot.) Ask children to make a tally mark in the table after each of ten spins.

Home Connection Ask your child to toss a number cube or spin a spinner. Tally the results.

E13

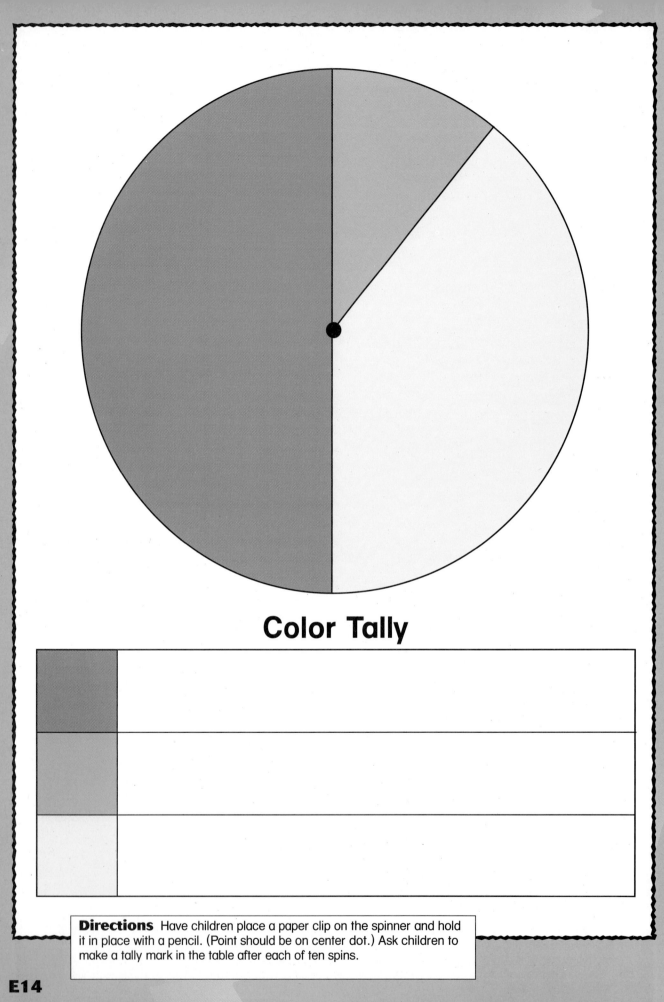

Color Tally

Directions Have children place a paper clip on the spinner and hold it in place with a pencil. (Point should be on center dot.) Ask children to make a tally mark in the table after each of ten spins.

Name _____

1

```
5    6    7
```

2

```
6    7    8
```

3

_____   7   _____   _____   _____

4

5

Heads or Tails?

(penny heads)	| | | |
(penny tails)	| | | | | |

Directions Have children: **1.** and **2.** circle the number of muffins, **3.** write the numbers 6 to 10 in order, **4.** circle the sixth cookie and mark an X on the ninth cookie, **5.** look at the table, and then circle the group with fewer tally marks.

Name _____

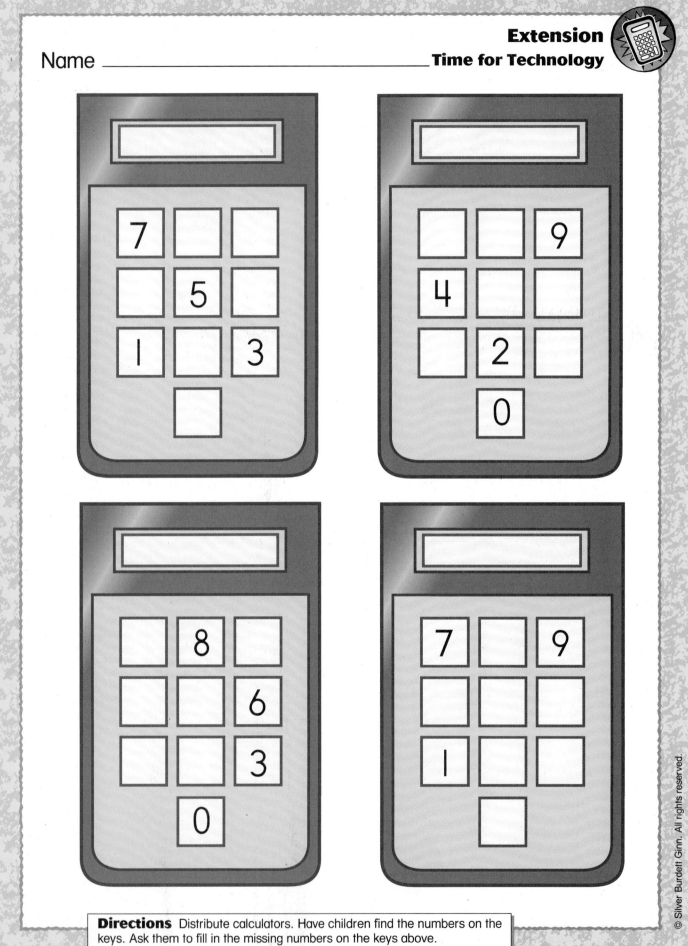

Directions Distribute calculators. Have children find the numbers on the keys. Ask them to fill in the missing numbers on the keys above.

CHAPTER 6

Measurement

I'm a Builder

A Note to the Family

During the next few weeks, your child will be learning about measurement. Here are some learning ideas you can share together.

At-Home Activities

- Cut three different lengths of string or ribbon. Ask your child to put them in order from shortest to longest.

- Collect a feather, a book, and a chair (or three other objects that have different weights). Ask your child which is the lightest and which is the heaviest.

- Fill two bowls or jars of different sizes with water and have your child identify which bowl holds more and which holds less.

Read About It!

To read more with your child about measurement, look for these books in your local library.

- *Bruno the Carpenter* by Lars Klinting (Henry Holt, 1995)
- *Inch by Inch* by Leo Lionni (Mulberry, 1995)
- *How Big Is a Foot?* by Rolf Myller (Dell, 1990)

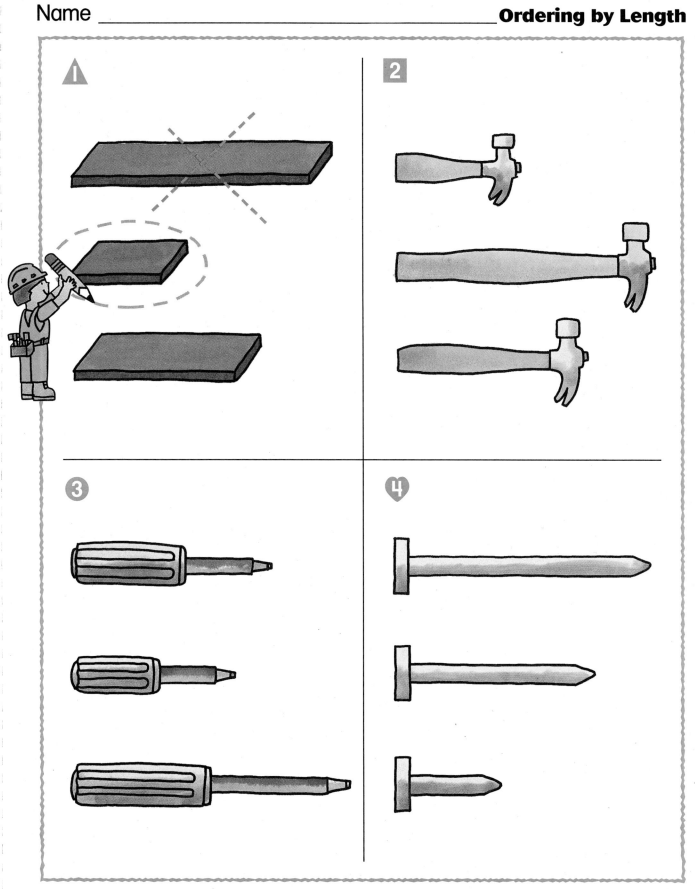

Directions Have children order the objects from shortest to longest by circling the shortest item and crossing out the longest item.

Home Connection Give your child three spoons of different lengths. Ask which is the longest and which is the shortest.

F3

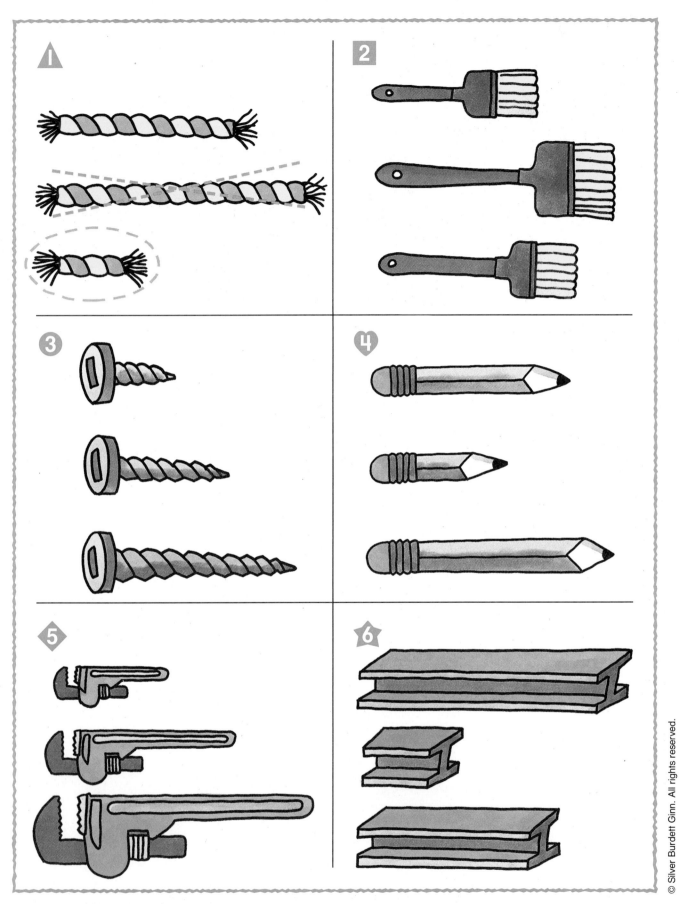

Directions Have children order the objects from shortest to longest by circling the shortest item and crossing out the longest item.

F4

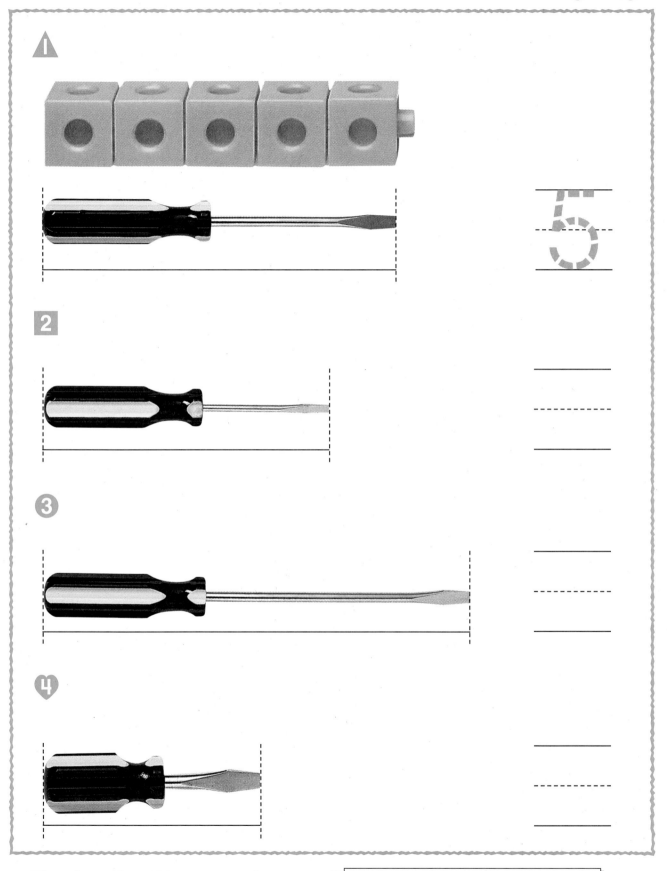

1

5

2

3

4

Directions Have children use snap cubes to measure the length of each screwdriver. Have them write each measure.

Home Connection Using a small object, such as a paper clip, have your child measure the length of kitchen utensils.

F5

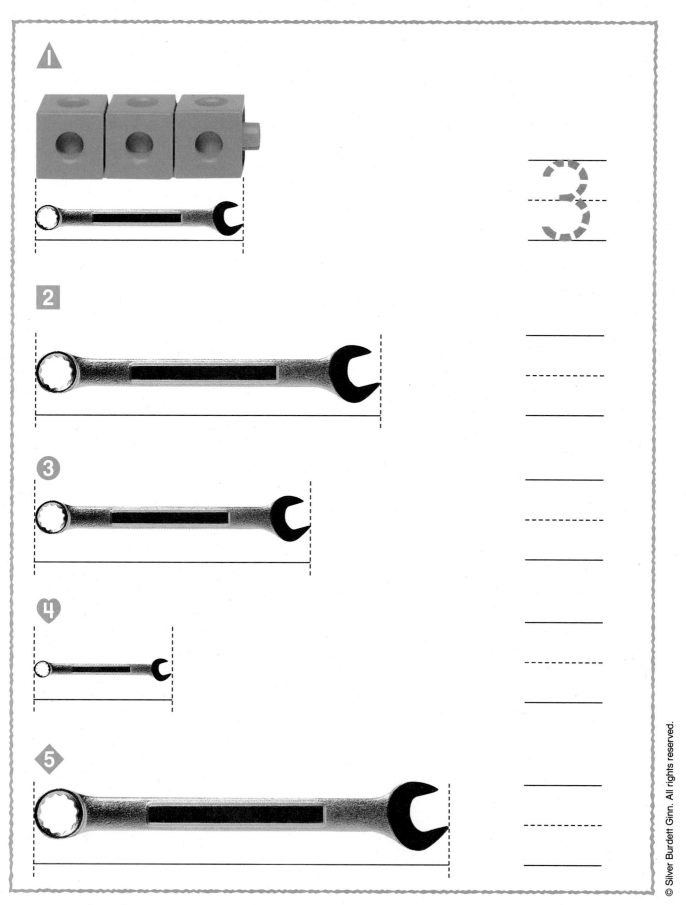

Directions Have children use snap cubes to measure the length of each wrench. Have them write each measure.

F6

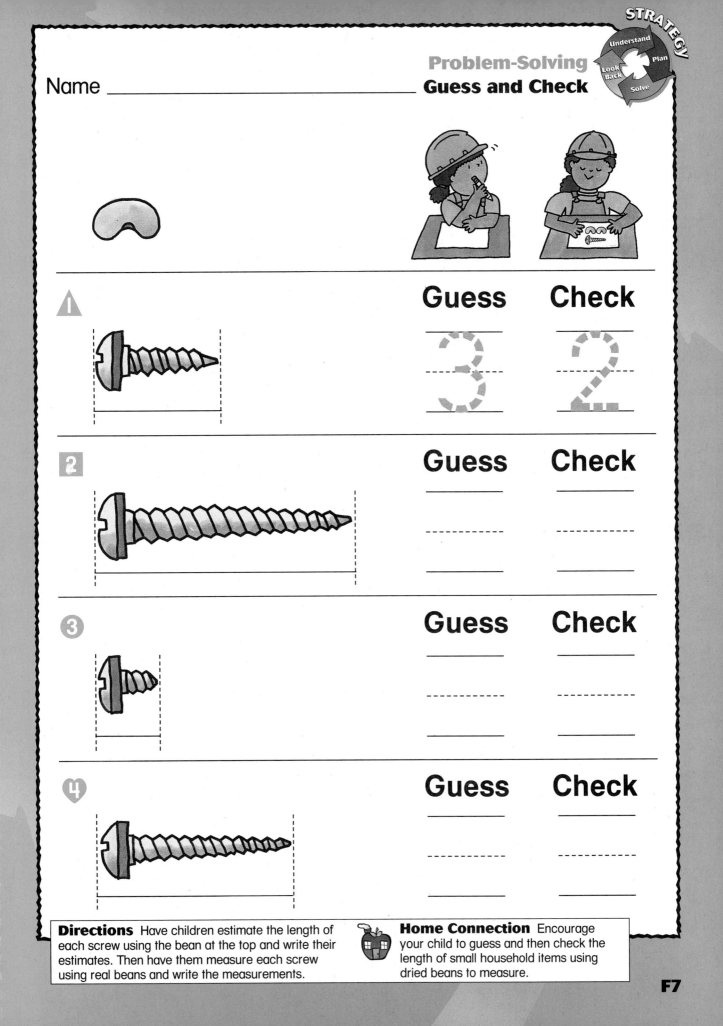

Problem-Solving
Guess and Check

STRATEGY
Understand
Plan
Solve
Look Back

Name _____

Guess **Check**

1. 3 2

Guess **Check**

2.

Guess **Check**

3.

Guess **Check**

4.

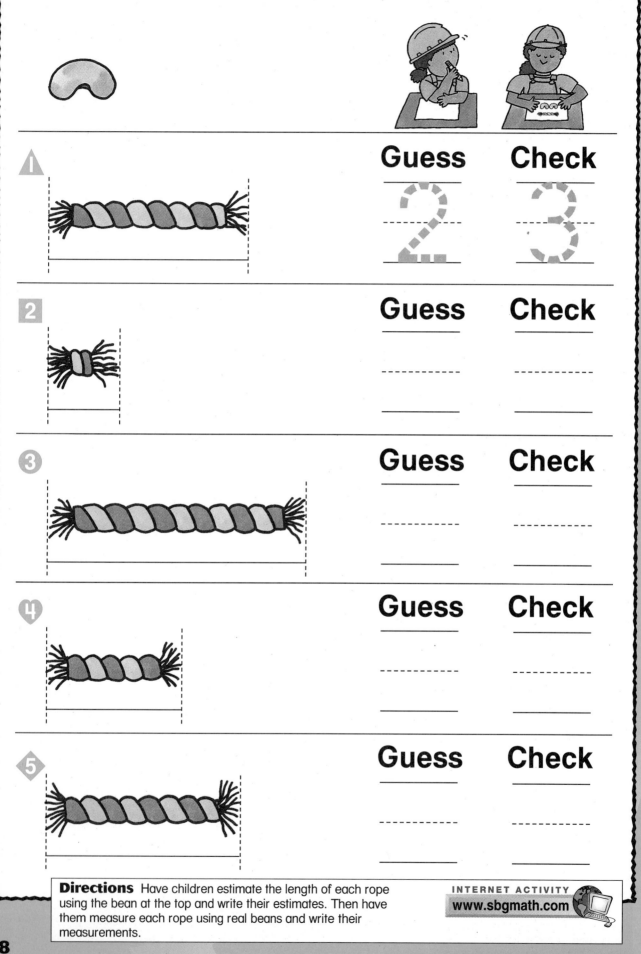

1

Guess   Check

2   3

2

Guess   Check

3

Guess   Check

4

Guess   Check

5

Guess   Check

Directions Have children estimate the length of each rope using the bean at the top and write their estimates. Then have them measure each rope using real beans and write their measurements.

INTERNET ACTIVITY
www.sbgmath.com

F8

Name _____ **Ordering by Weight**

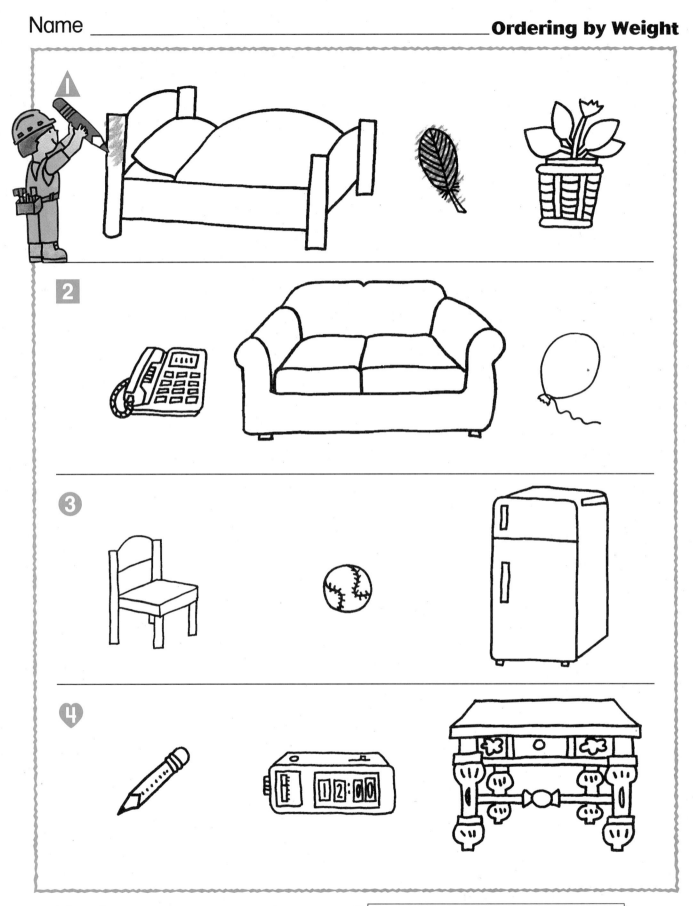

Directions Have children order the household objects in each exercise by coloring the heaviest one blue and the lightest one red.

Home Connection Help your child put three objects of different weights, such as a feather, a toy, and a large bowl, in order from lightest to heaviest.

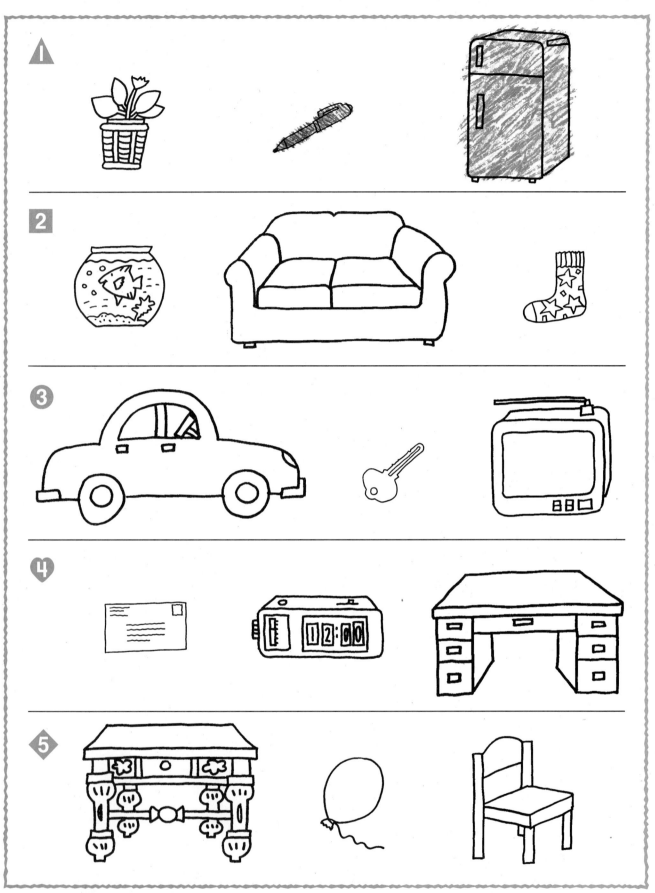

Directions Have children order the household objects in each exercise by coloring the heaviest one blue and the lightest one red.

F10

Name _____

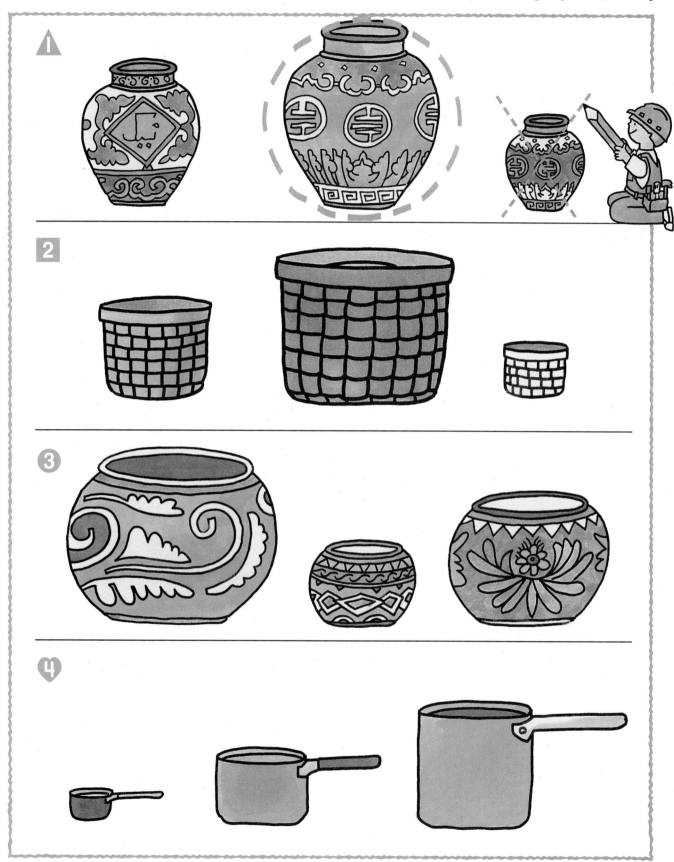

1

2

3

4

Directions In each exercise, have children mark an X on the container that can hold the least and circle the container that can hold the most.

Home Connection Help your child find three jars and experiment to determine which holds the least cotton balls.

F11

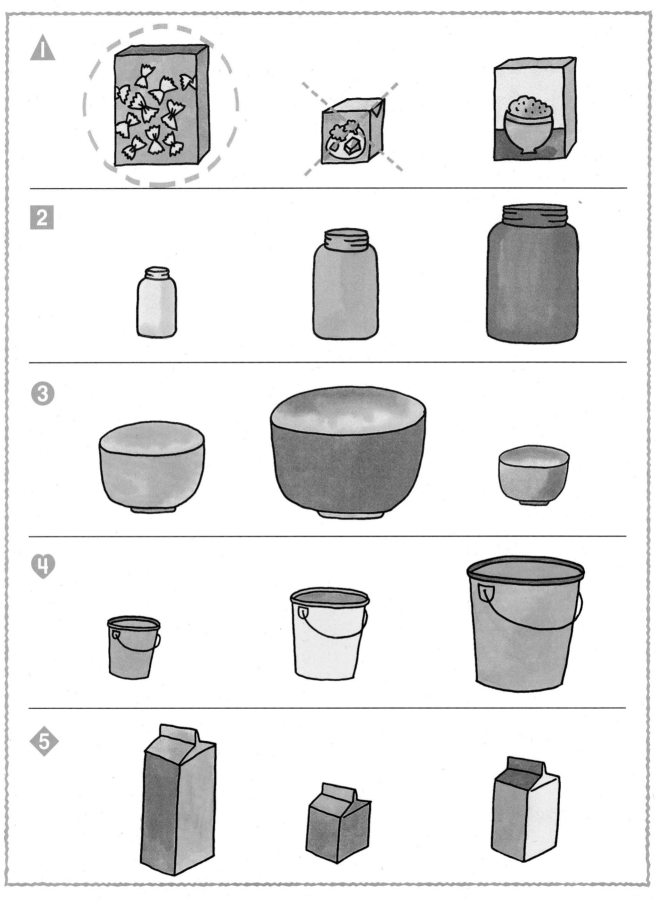

Directions In each exercise, have children mark an X on the container that can hold the least and circle the container that can hold the most.

F12

How much does it hold?

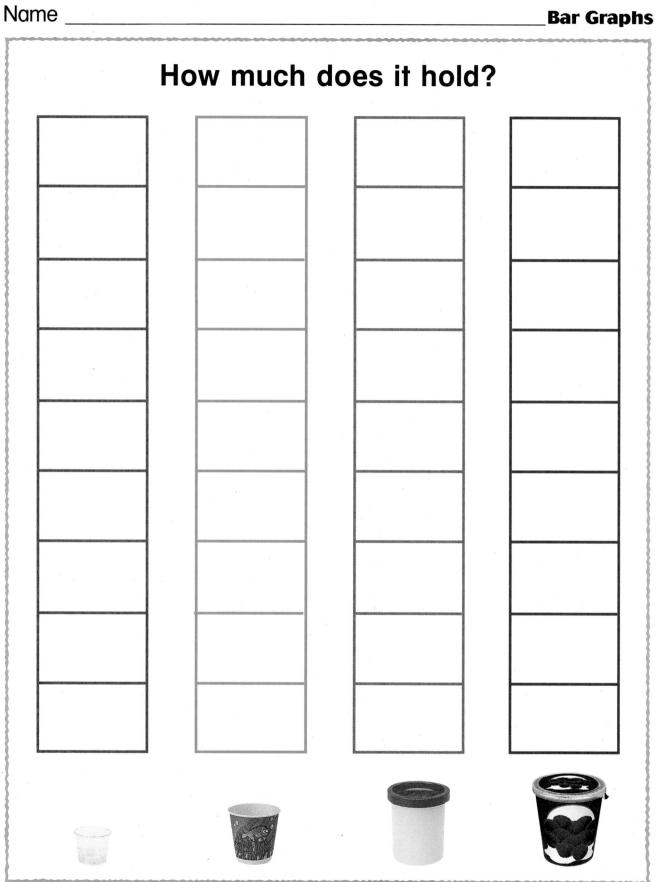

Directions Have children find the pictured containers in the classroom and fill each with loose snap cubes. Have them color the same number of squares in the graph as snap cubes in the container.

Home Connection Have your child fill a bowl and a cup with cotton balls. Help him or her figure out which container can hold more cotton balls.

How long is it?

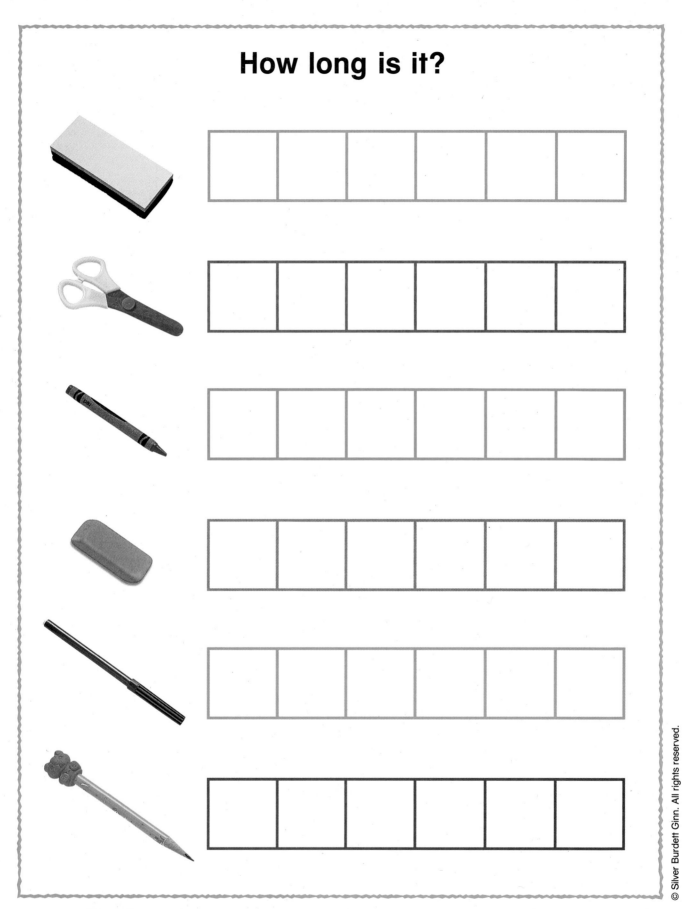

Directions Have children find the pictured objects in the classroom and
then measure each one with snap cubes. Have them color the same
number of squares as cubes.

F14

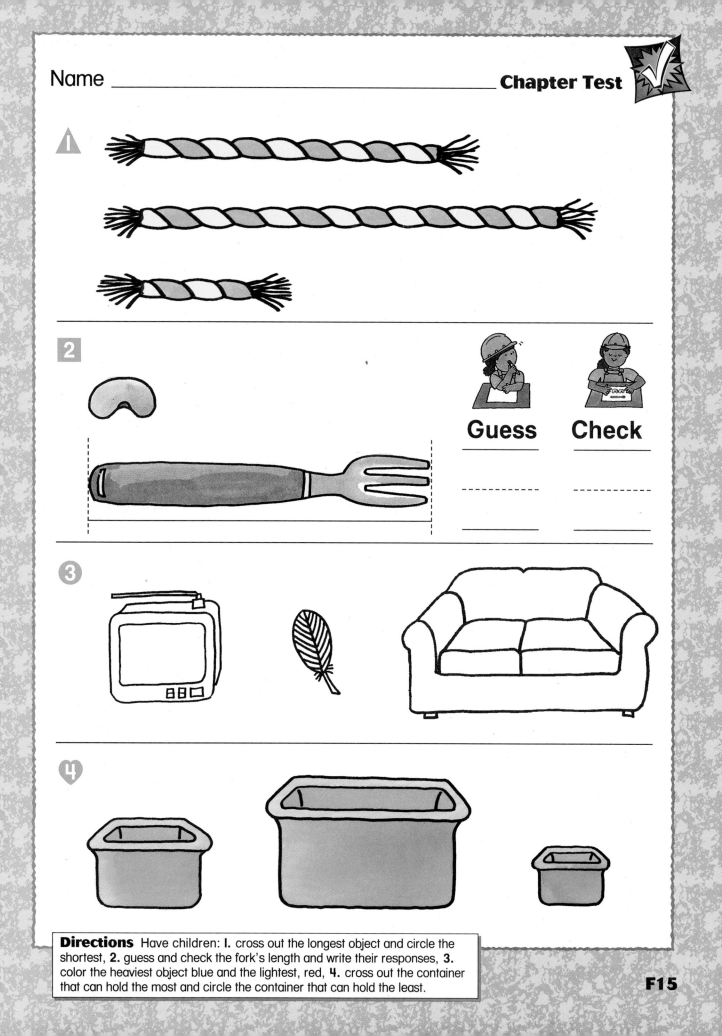

1

2

Guess   Check

3

4

Directions Have children: **1.** cross out the longest object and circle the shortest, **2.** guess and check the fork's length and write their responses, **3.** color the heaviest object blue and the lightest, red, **4.** cross out the container that can hold the most and circle the container that can hold the least.

Name _____

1

2

3

4

Directions Have children compare each pair of pictures and thermometers. Have them circle the picture where the temperature looks hotter.

CHAPTER 7

Time and Money

I'm a Postal Worker

A Note to the Family

During the next few weeks, your child will be learning about time and money. Here are some learning ideas you can share together.

At-Home Activities

- Ask your child to name activities that are usually done during the day. Then ask him or her to name activities usually done at night.

- Using a clock with hands (and a digital clock at the same time, if possible), ask your child to look at the clock and tell you the time. Ask only when the clock is showing time to the hour (for example, five o'clock).

- Give your child a pile of pennies, nickels, and dimes. Have him or her sort them by type of coin. Ask your child to tell you how many cents each type of coin is worth.

- Collect pennies in a bank. Then set out groups of up to ten pennies. Ask your child to trade pennies for nickels (five cents) and dimes (ten cents).

Read About It!

To read more with your child about time and money, look for these books in your local library.

- *Now Soon Later* by Lisa Grunwald (Greenwillow, 1996)
- *Time to Wake Up!* by Marisabina Russo (Greenwillow, 1994)
- *Jelly Beans for Sale* by Bruce McMillan (Scholastic, 1996)

Problem-Solving
Use Logical Reasoning

STRATEGY
Understand
Plan
Look Back
Solve

Name _____

①

_ _ _ 3 _ _ _ 2 _ _ _ 1

②

_ _ _ _ _ _ _ _ _ _ _ _

③

_ _ _ _ _ _ _ _ _ _ _ _

Directions Have children order the events from first to last by writing 1, 2, and 3.

Home Connection Choose three activities, such as eating dinner, brushing teeth, and going to bed. Ask your child to identify which happens first, next, and last.

G3

Directions In each exercise, have children draw a line from the top picture to the picture that shows what happens next.

G4

Name _____

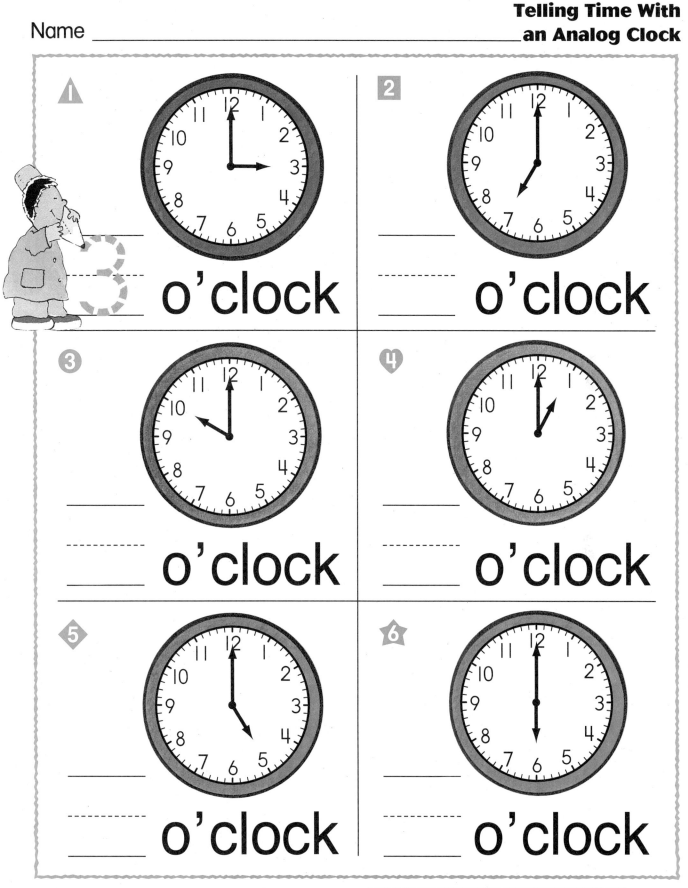

1. ____ o'clock

2. ____ o'clock

3. ____ o'clock

4. ____ o'clock

5. ____ o'clock

6. ____ o'clock

Directions Have children write the time shown
on each clock.

Home Connection Just before a
favorite television show that begins on
the hour, ask your child to look at a clock
and tell you the time.

G5

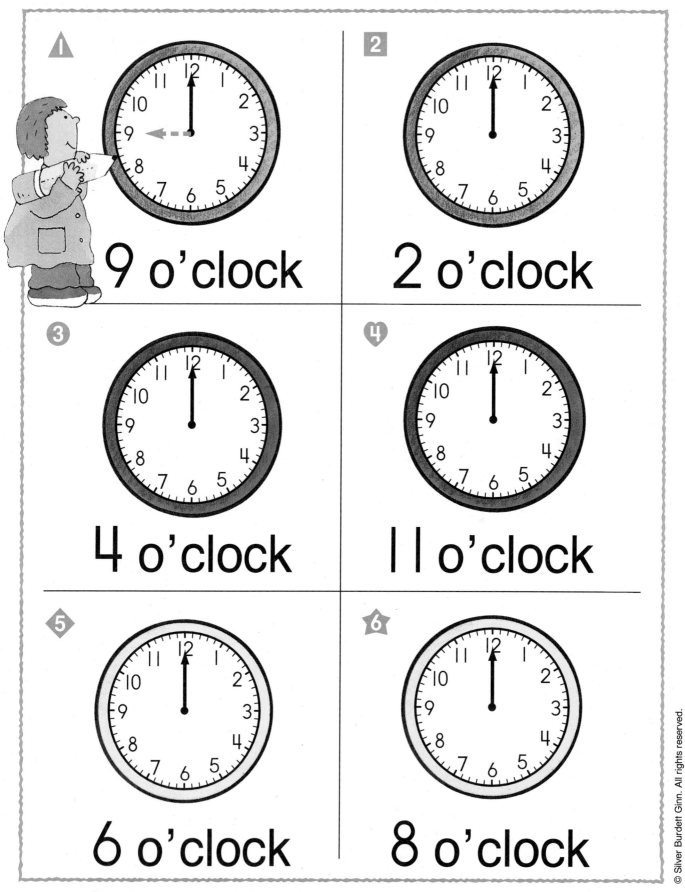

1 9 o'clock

2 2 o'clock

3 4 o'clock

4 11 o'clock

5 6 o'clock

6 8 o'clock

Directions Have children draw each hour hand to show the correct time.

G6

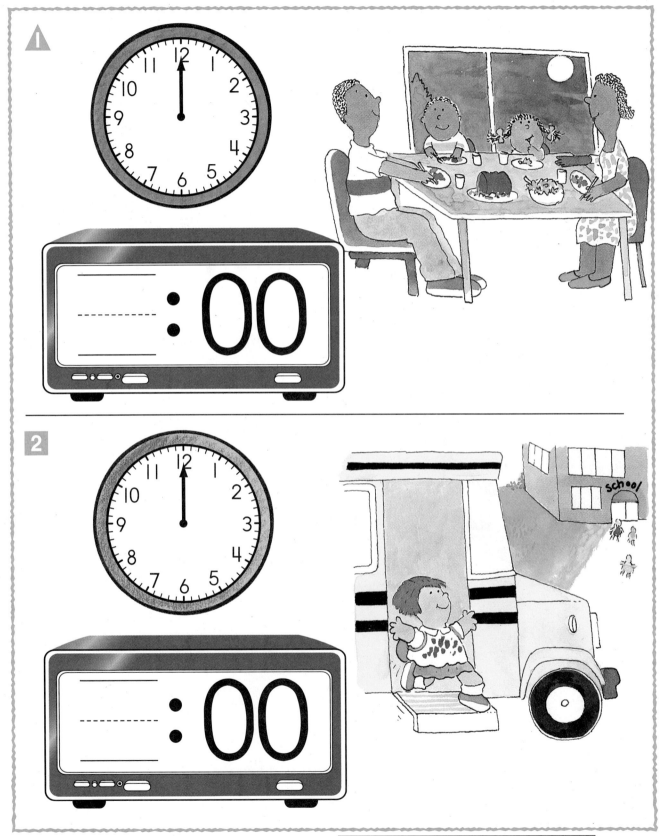

1

2

Directions Have children draw the hour hand on the analog clock and write the hour on the digital clock to show the time at which each pictured activity might have happened.

Home Connection Show your child a digital clock. Ask him or her to point to the numbers that show hours and the numbers that show minutes.

Directions Have children look at each analog clock. Ask them to write the hour on the digital clock to show the same time.

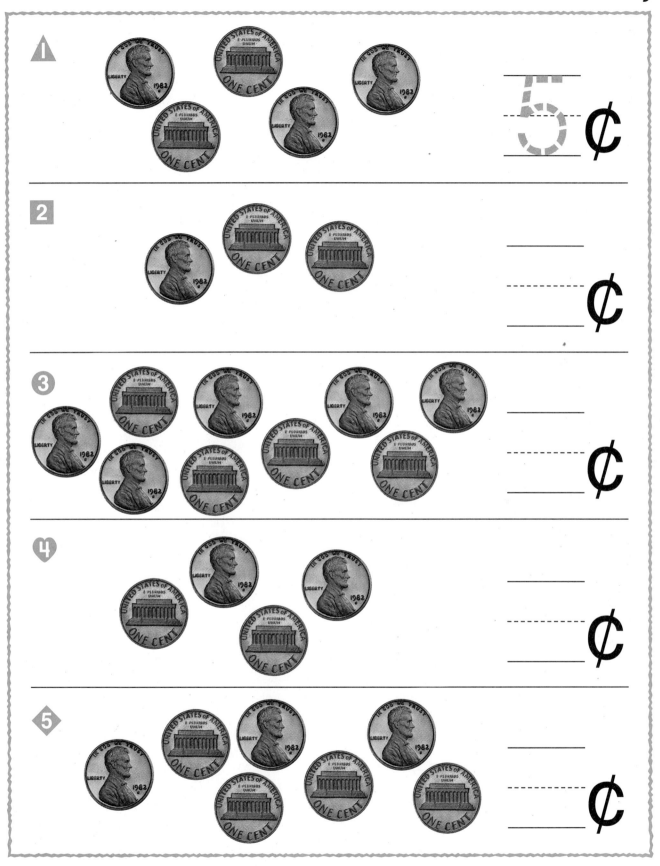

1 __5__ ¢

2 _____ ¢

3 _____ ¢

4 _____ ¢

5 _____ ¢

Directions Ask children to count the pennies. Have them record the value of the group by writing the number.

Home Connection Give your child a few pennies. Have him or her count them and tell you how many cents there are.

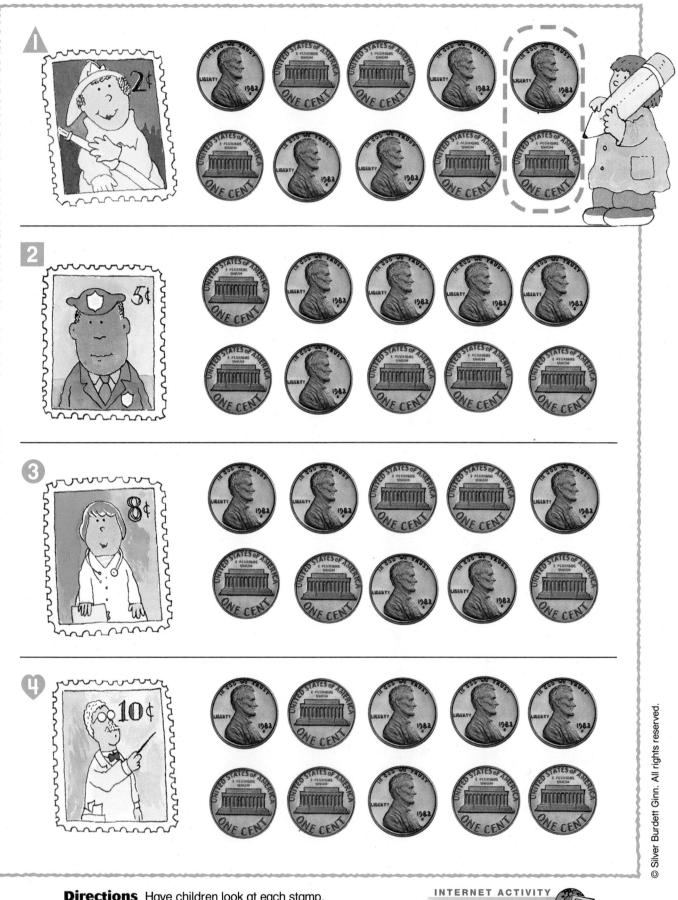

Directions Have children look at each stamp.
Have them circle the pennies needed to buy that stamp.

INTERNET ACTIVITY
www.sbgmath.com

G10

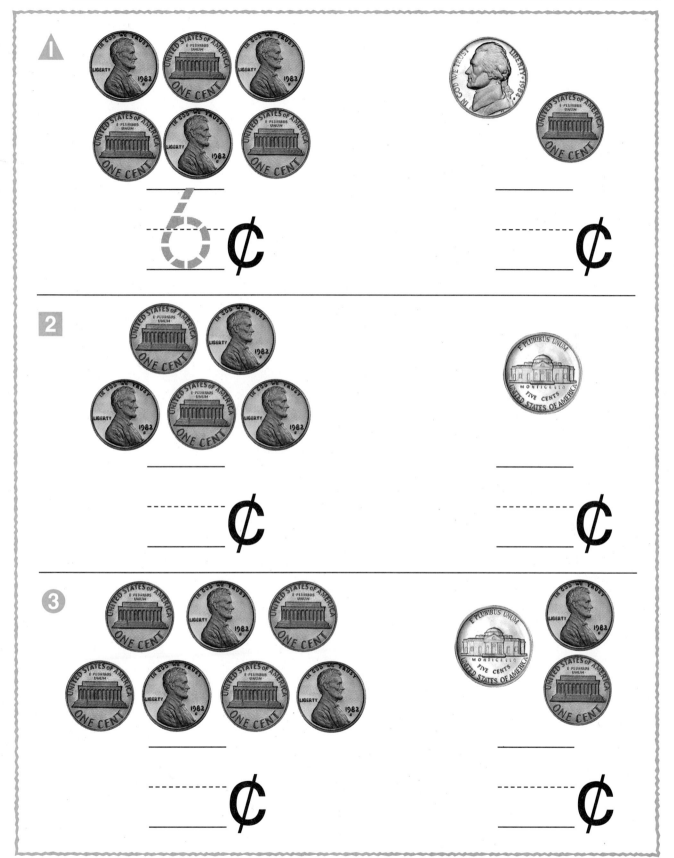

1

_____6_____ ¢

_____ ¢

2

_____ ¢

_____ ¢

3

_____ ¢

_____ ¢

Directions Ask children to figure out how many cents each group of coins shows. Have them write the number.

 Home Connection Give your child one nickel and seven pennies. Ask him or her to show you how many pennies can be traded for a nickel.

G11

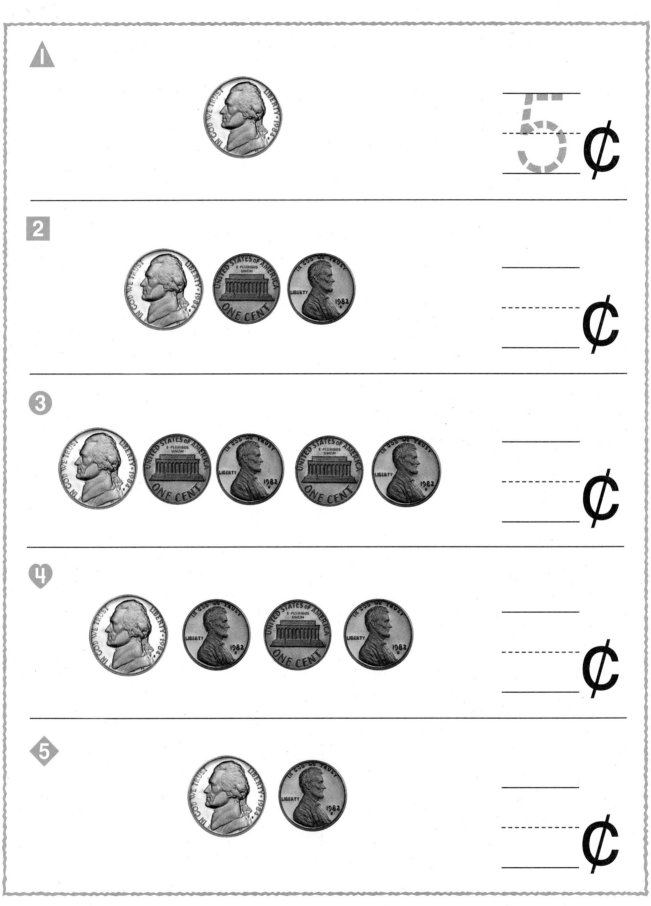

1		5¢
2		___¢
3		___¢
4		___¢
5		___¢

Directions Have children figure out how many cents each group of coins shows. Have them write the number.

G12

Name _____ **Dime**

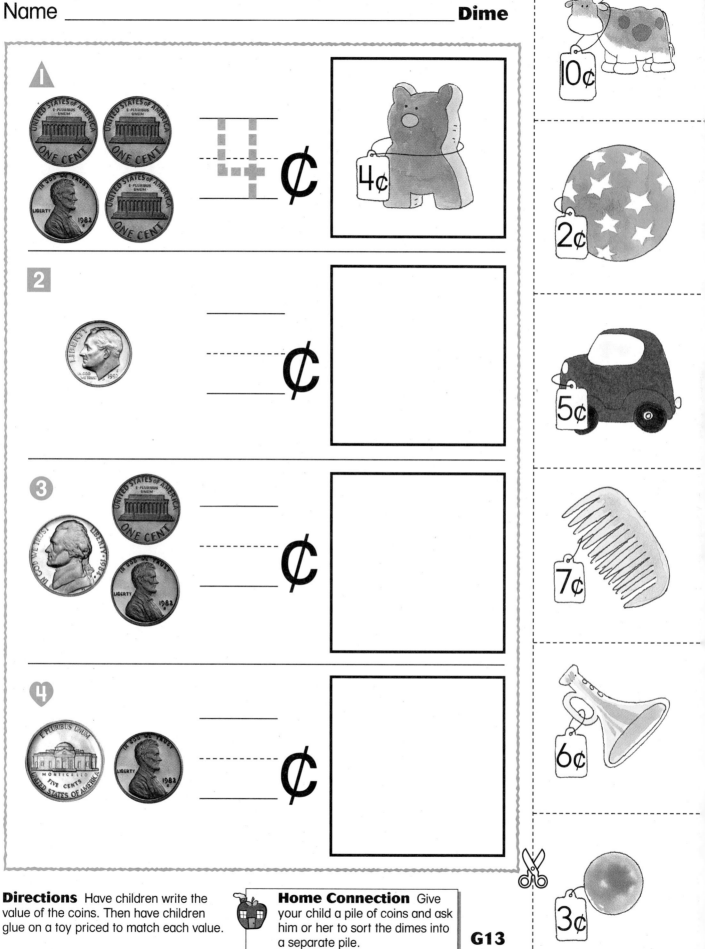

1. ____ ____ | 4¢
2. ____ ____ | ¢
3. ____ ____ | ¢
4. ____ ____ | ¢

10¢

2¢

5¢

7¢

6¢

3¢

Directions Have children write the value of the coins. Then have children glue on a toy priced to match each value.

Home Connection Give your child a pile of coins and ask him or her to sort the dimes into a separate pile.

G13

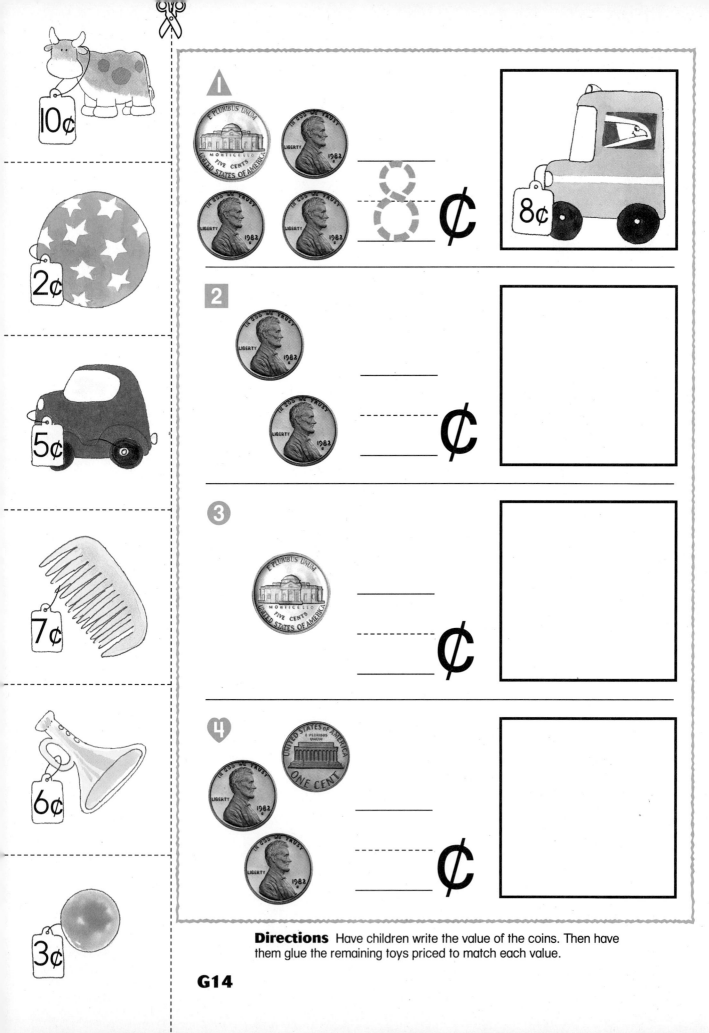

1

_____
_ _ _ _
8 ¢

8¢

2

_____
_ _ _ _
____ ¢

3

_____
_ _ _ _
____ ¢

4

_____
_ _ _ _
____ ¢

10¢

2¢

5¢

7¢

6¢

3¢

Directions Have children write the value of the coins. Then have them glue the remaining toys priced to match each value.

G14

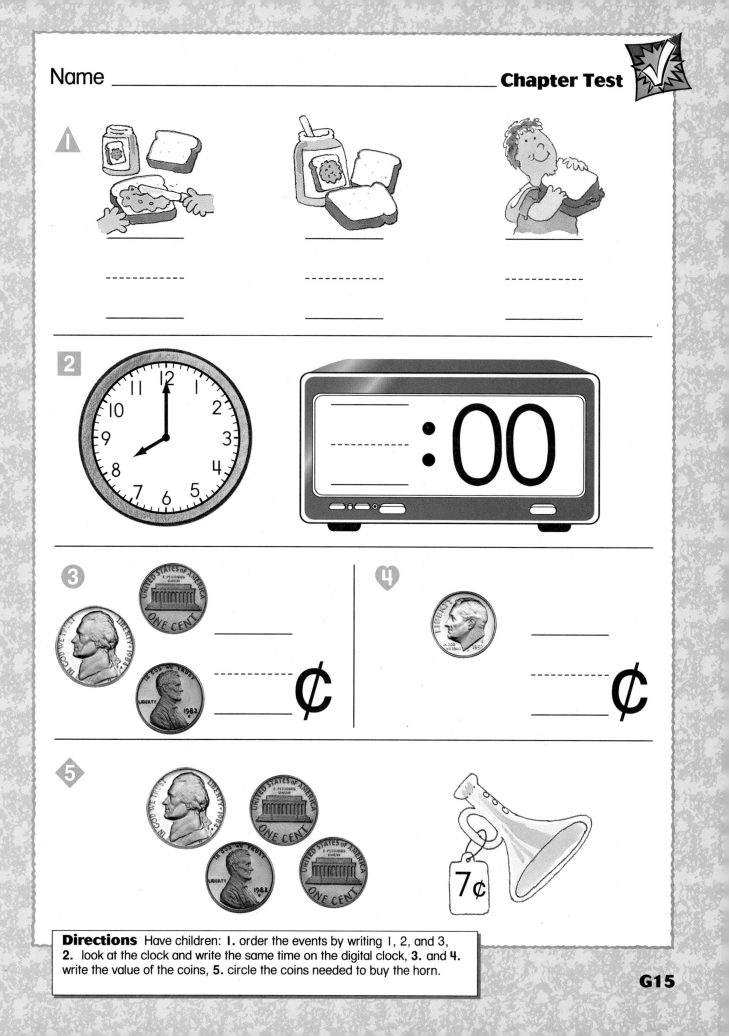

1

- - - - - - - - - -   - - - - - - - - - -   - - - - - - - - - -

_____   _____   _____

2

_____ : **00**
- - - - - - - -

3

_____
- - - - - - - - ¢

4

_____
- - - - - - - - ¢

5

7¢

Directions Have children: **1.** order the events by writing 1, 2, and 3, **2.** look at the clock and write the same time on the digital clock, **3.** and **4.** write the value of the coins, **5.** circle the coins needed to buy the horn.

G15

Name _____

25¢   25¢

Directions Have children mark an X on every quarter.

G16

CHAPTER 8

Exploring Greater Numbers

I'm a Teacher

A Note to the Family

During the next few weeks, your child will be learning about numbers greater than 10. Here are some learning ideas you can share together.

 ### At-Home Activities

- The next time you and your child climb a flight of stairs together, have him or her count the steps as you climb.

- On trips to the supermarket, ask your child to look for the numbers 11 through 20 on food labels and price tags.

- Show your child a calendar page. Name a number that is on the calendar and ask your child to point to it. Many calendars have one page that shows all the months together. Help your child count how many months are in a year.

 ### Read About It!

To read more with your child about numbers greater than 10, look for these books in your local library.

- *Counting Wildflowers* by Bruce McMillan (Mulberry/Lothrop, Lee & Shepard, 1995)

- *One Potato* by Diana Pomeroy (Harcourt Brace, 1996)

- *From One to One Hundred* by Teri Sloat (Dutton Children's Books, 1991)

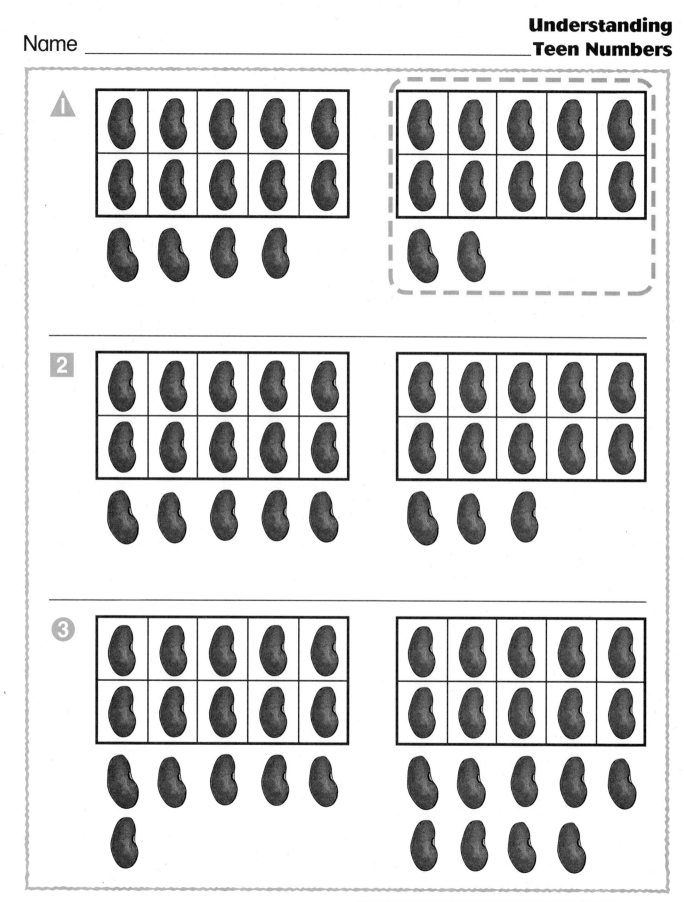

Directions Have children circle the group that shows 12 beans in exercise 1, the group that shows 15 beans in exercise 2, and the group that shows 19 beans in exercise 3.

Home Connection Give your child 15 cereal pieces. Have him or her arrange them in rows of five. Ask, "Are there more than ten pieces?"

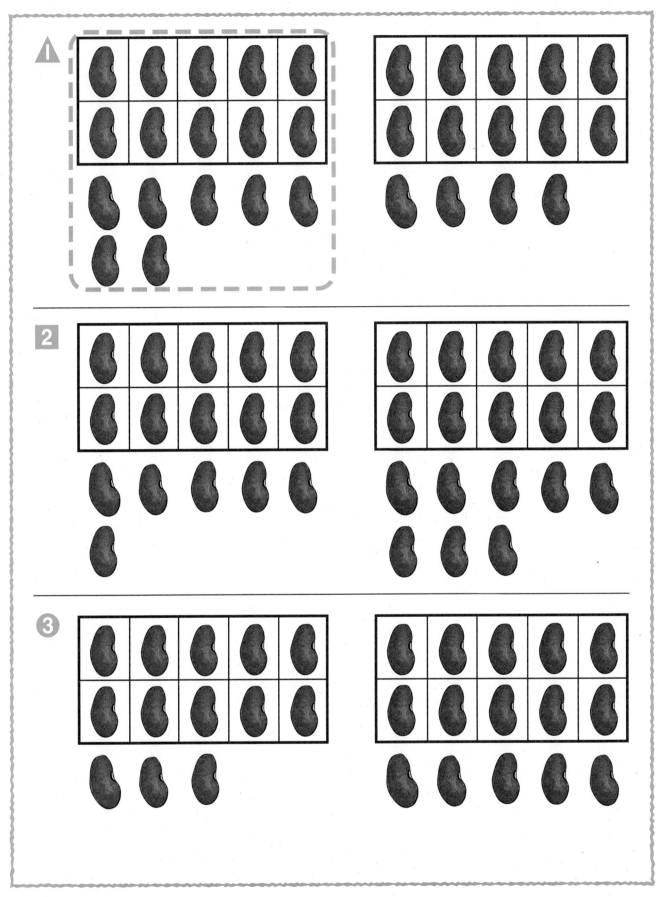

Directions Have children circle the group that shows 17 beans in exercise 1, the group that shows 18 beans in exercise 2, and the group that shows 13 beans in exercise 3.

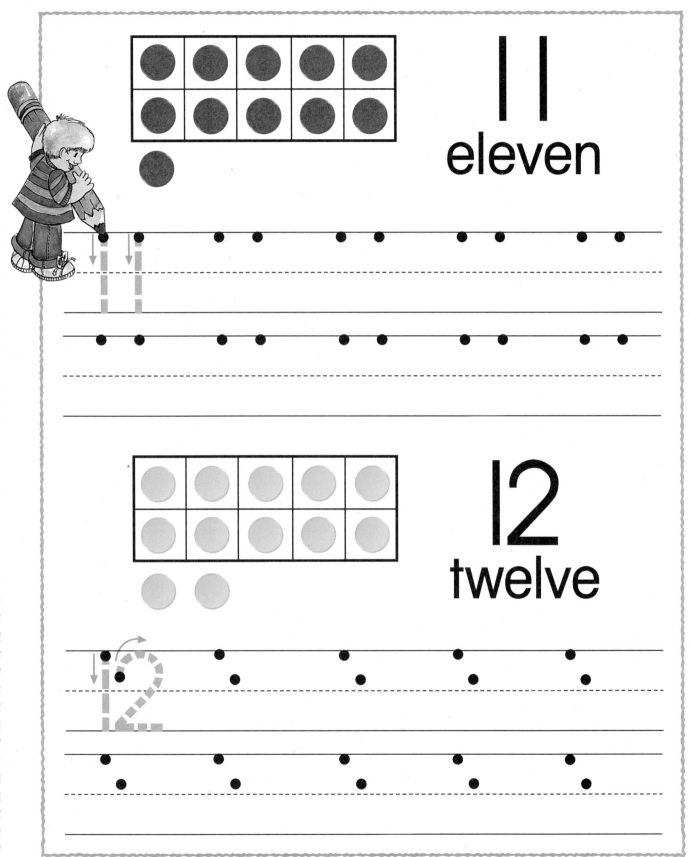

11
eleven

12
twelve

Directions Have children practice writing the numbers 11 and 12, beginning each number at the black dot.

Home Connection The next time you're at a store with your child, ask him or her to find the numbers 11, 12, 13, 14, and 15.

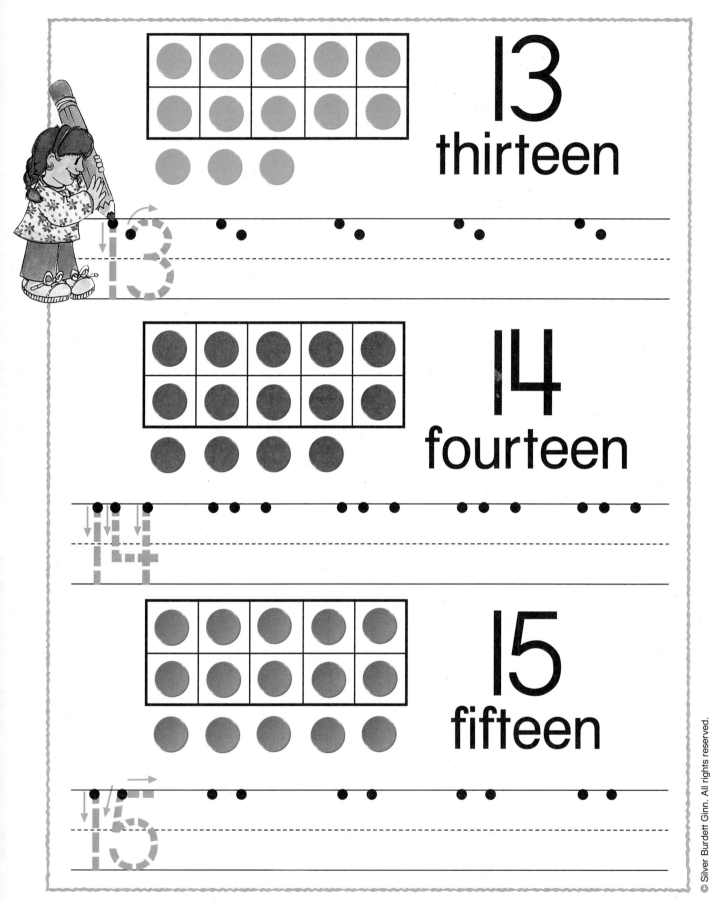

13 thirteen

14 fourteen

15 fifteen

Directions Have children practice writing the numbers 13, 14, and 15, beginning each number at the black dot.

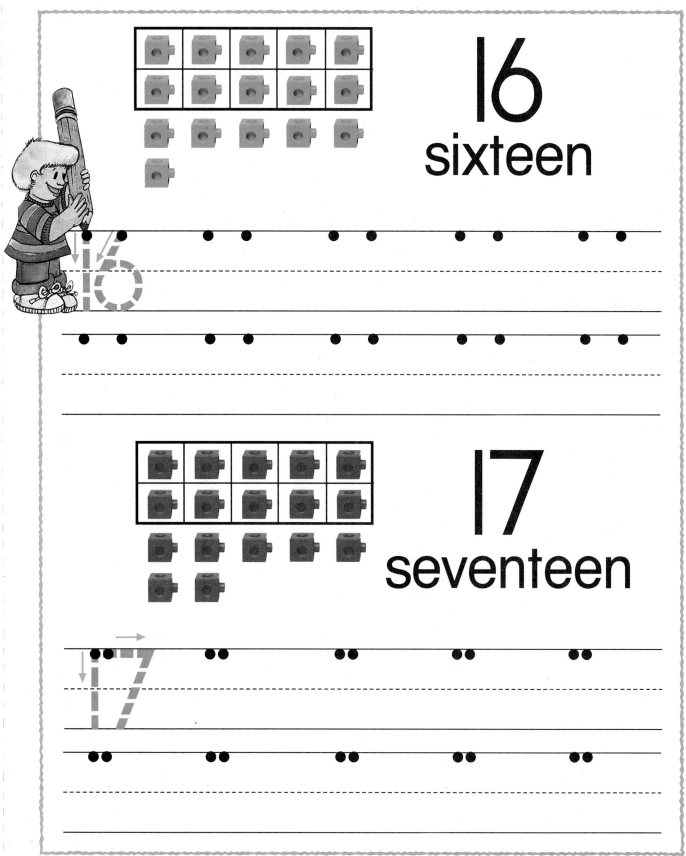

16
sixteen

17
seventeen

Directions Have children practice writing the numbers 16 and 17, beginning each number at the black dot.

Home Connection On your next walk or ride with your child, ask him or her to find the numbers 16, 17, 18, 19, and 20 on signs or billboards.

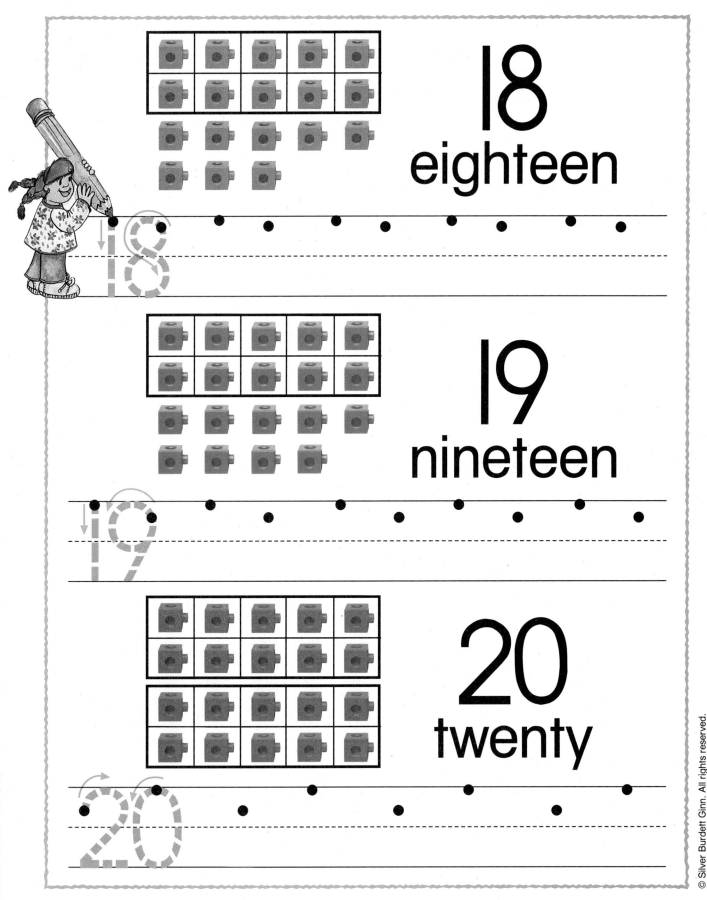

18
eighteen

19
nineteen

20
twenty

Directions Have children practice writing the numbers 18, 19, and 20, beginning each number at the black dot.

H8

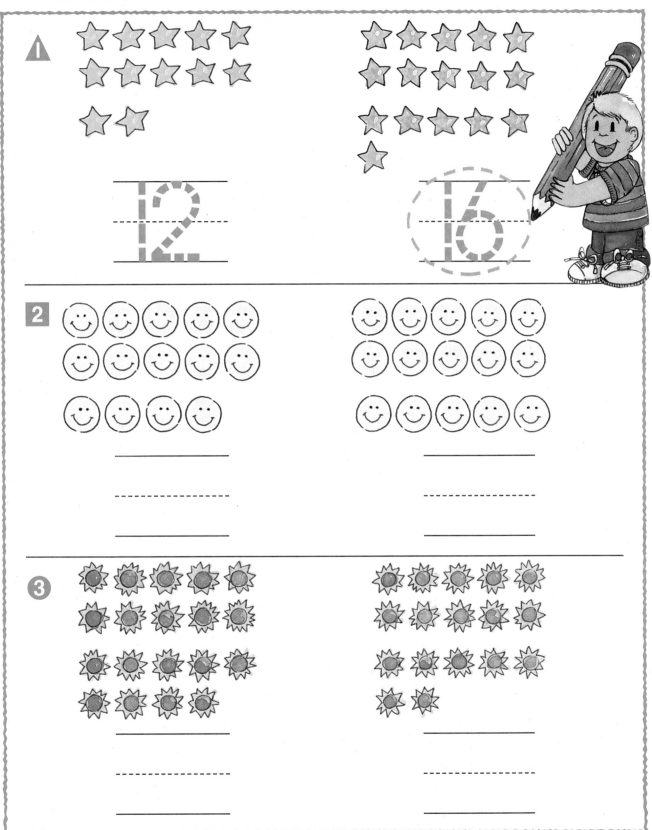

Directions Have children count each group of objects and write the number. Ask them to circle the number for the group that has more objects.

Home Connection Make two groups of small objects, such as 12 crackers and 16 crackers. Ask your child, "Which group has more crackers?"

1

18   17

2

_____   _____

- - - - - - -   - - - - - - -

_____   _____

3

_____   _____

- - - - - - -   - - - - - - -

_____   _____

Directions Have children count each group of objects and write the number. Ask them to circle the number for the group that has fewer objects.

INTERNET ACTIVITY
www.sbgmath.com

H10

Name _____

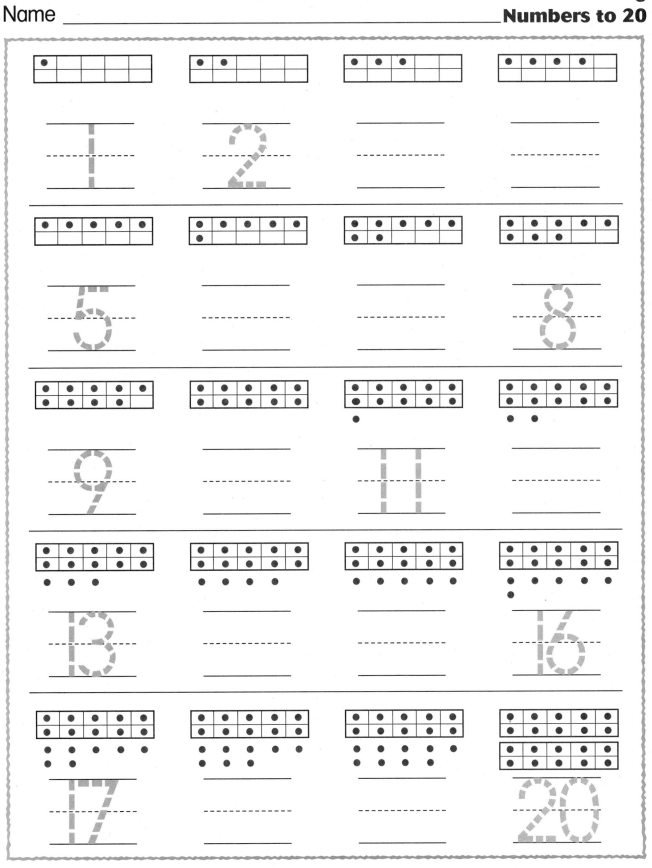

Directions Have children either trace or write the missing numbers.

Home Connection Write the numbers 16 through 20 on a piece of paper. Cut them apart and ask your child to put them in order.

H11

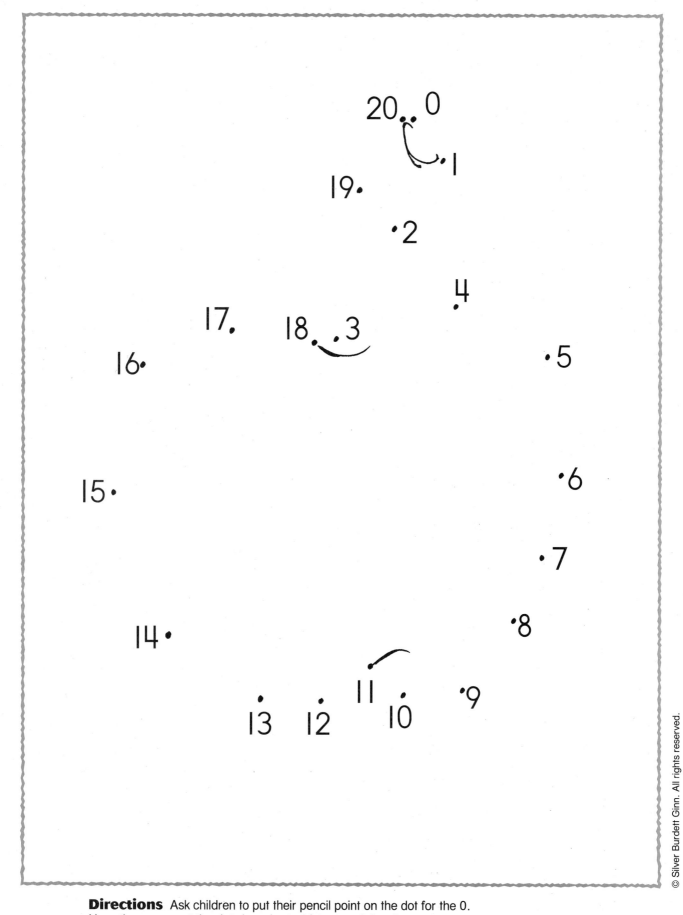

Directions Ask children to put their pencil point on the dot for the 0.
Have them connect the dots in order to 20 to reveal the picture.

Problem-Solving
Find a Pattern

STRATEGY
Understand
Plan
Look Back
Solve

Name _____

MARCH

Sunday	Monday	Tuesday	Wednesday	Thursday	Friday	Saturday
1	2	3	4	5	6	7
8	9	10	11	12	13	14
15	16	17	18	19	20	21
22	23	24	25	26	27	28
29	30	31				

Directions Have children mark an X on these numbers: 2, 9, 16, 23. Have them tell the pattern, then mark the number that comes next.

Home Connection Show your child a calendar and have him or her find the number 20 in every month. Repeat with other numbers from 1 to 31.

H13

AUGUST

Sunday	Monday	Tuesday	Wednesday	Thursday	Friday	Saturday
1	2	3	4	5	6	7
8	9	10	11	12	13	14
15	16	17	18	19	20	21
22	23	24	25	26	27	28
29	30	31				

Directions Have children first identify then color the numbers between 21 and 29. Then have them tell the pattern.

Name _____

1

2

17

3

4

21	22	23	24	25	26	27	28	29	30

Directions Have children: **1.** circle the group that shows 14, **2.** write the numbers 17 to 20 in order, **3.** circle the group that has more objects **4.** mark an X on 23 and 27; color in a pattern to show skip counting by twos from 22.

Our Favorite Recess Activities

Activity	Tallies ⅲ = 5	Number
		_____ ------------------ _____
		_____ ------------------ _____
		_____ ------------------ _____

Directions Ask children, "Is the sandbox your favorite recess activity?"
Model making tally marks, including groups of five, to record responses.
Then have children copy the tally marks and write the number. Repeat for
each activity.

A Note to the Family

During the next few weeks, your child will be learning about addition. Here are some learning ideas you can share together.

At-Home Activities

- Place six dried beans or pieces of pasta on a flat surface, and ask your child to count them aloud. Have him or her separate the items into two piles and then count all of them again. Encourage your child to repeat the activity, creating different piles each time to see that six items are always six items, no matter how they are arranged.

- Help your child use stuffed animals to act out joining problems. For example: *Two animals are having a party. Three more animals join them.* Ask your child: *How many animals are at the party altogether?*

- Using pennies, create addition problems for your child to solve. For example, put two pennies in one pile and two pennies in another. Ask your child to put the piles together and tell how many pennies there are in all. You might have your child save the pennies in a piggy bank.

Read About It!

To read more about addition with your child, look for these books in your local library.

- *Fish Eyes: A Book You Can Count On* by Lois Ehlert (Harcourt Brace Jovanovich, 1990)
- *Rhinos for Lunch and Elephants for Supper!* by Tololwa M. Mollel (Clarion, 1991)
- *One Gorilla* by Matthew Price (Farrar, Straus & Giroux, 1990)

Problem-Solving
Draw a Picture

STRATEGY
Understand
Plan
Solve
Look Back

Name _____

1

2

Directions Tell children the stories from Teacher Guide page 483. Have them draw pictures to solve the problems.

Home Connection Have your child draw a picture to solve this problem: "You have three apples. I give you two more. How many apples do you have in all?"

I3

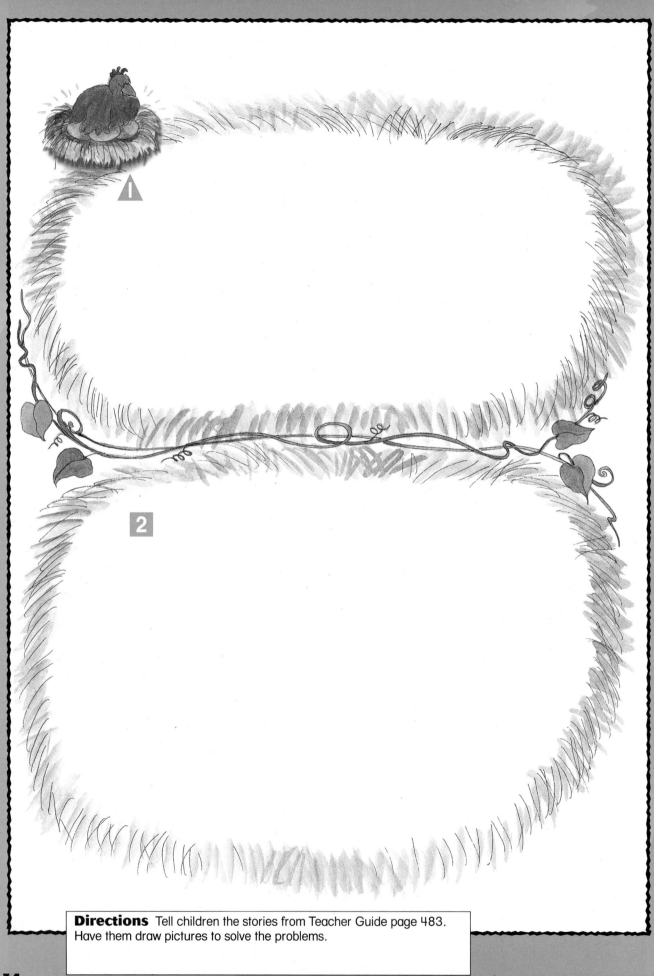

1

2

Directions Tell children the stories from Teacher Guide page 483.
Have them draw pictures to solve the problems.

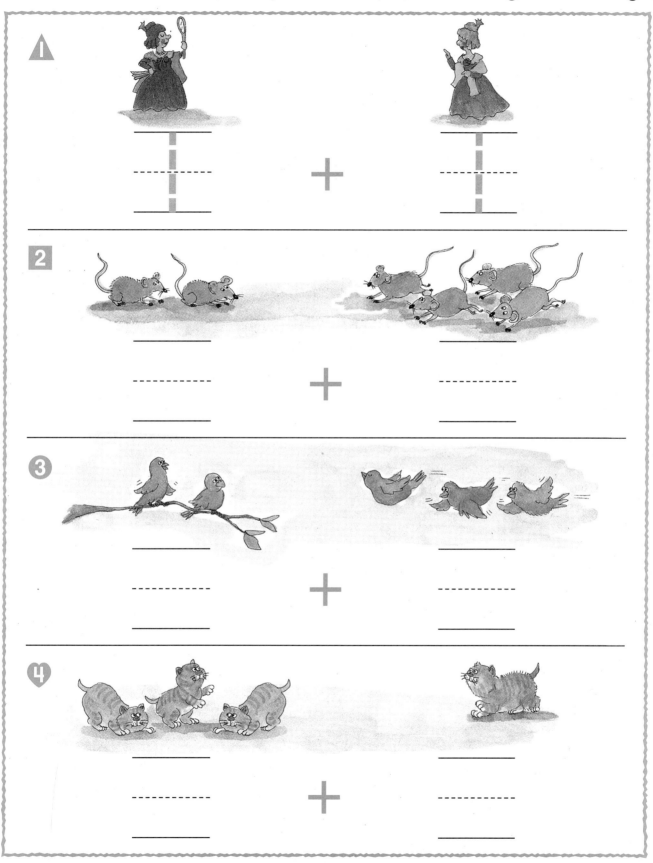

Directions Have children write how many there are in each group. Then have them tell how many there are in all.

Home Connection Make two groups of toys. Have your child count the toys in each group. Put them together and ask your child how many there are in all.

1 3 + 3

2 ___ + ___

3 ___ + ___

4 ___ + ___

Directions Have children write how many are in each group. Then have them tell how many there are in all.

16

1

1 + 4 =

2

5 + 1 =

3

1 + 3 =

4

4 + 2 =

Directions Ask children to look at the pictures.
Have them write the number in all.

Home Connection Ask your child
to use the pictures to tell addition stories,
such as, "One cat is on the mat. Four cats
join her. Now there are five cats in all."

17

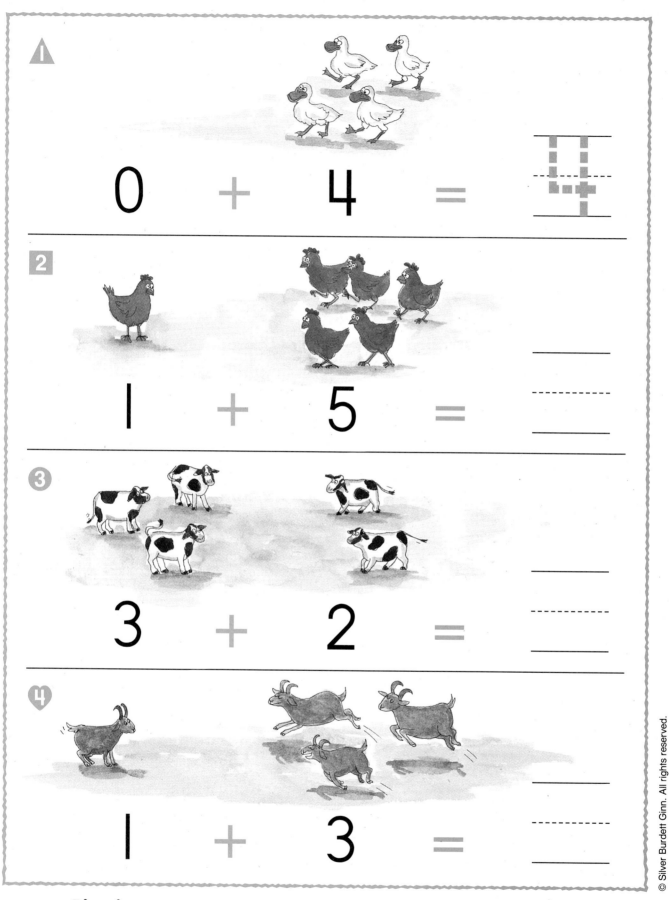

1. $0 + 4 =$ ____

2. $1 + 5 =$ ____

3. $3 + 2 =$ ____

4. $1 + 3 =$ ____

Directions Ask children to look at the pictures. Have them write the number in all.

I8

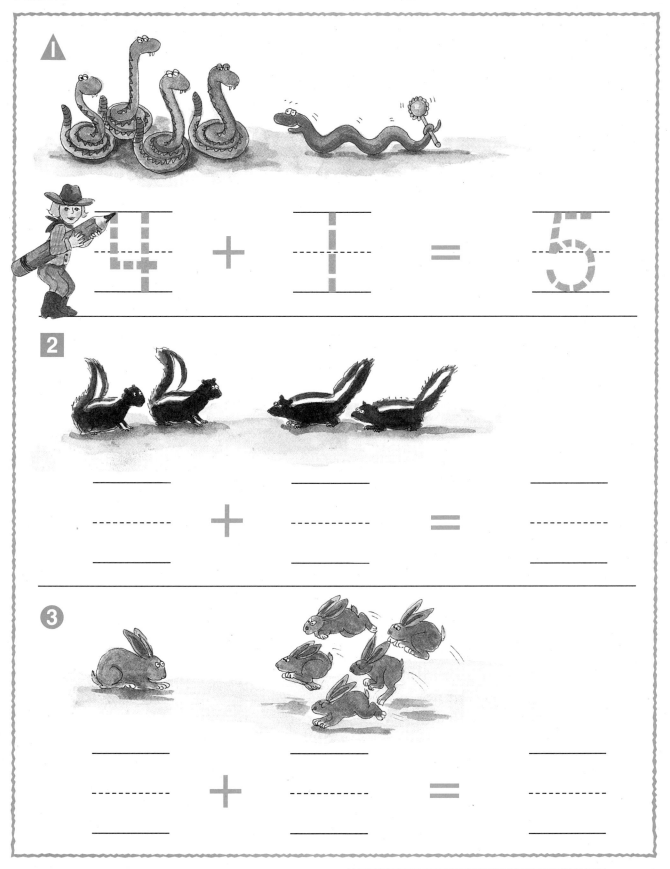

1

$$4 + 1 = 5$$

2

____ ____ ____

____ + ____ = ____

____ ____ ____

3

____ ____ ____

____ + ____ = ____

____ ____ ____

Directions Have children look at the pictures and then write the addition sentences.

Home Connection Help your child draw a picture to show 3 + 1 = 4.

I9

1

3 + 2 = 5

2

___ + ___ = ___

3

___ + ___ = ___

4

___ + ___ = ___

Directions Have children look at the pictures and then write the addition sentences.

INTERNET ACTIVITY
www.sbgmath.com

I10

Name _____ **Vertical Addition**

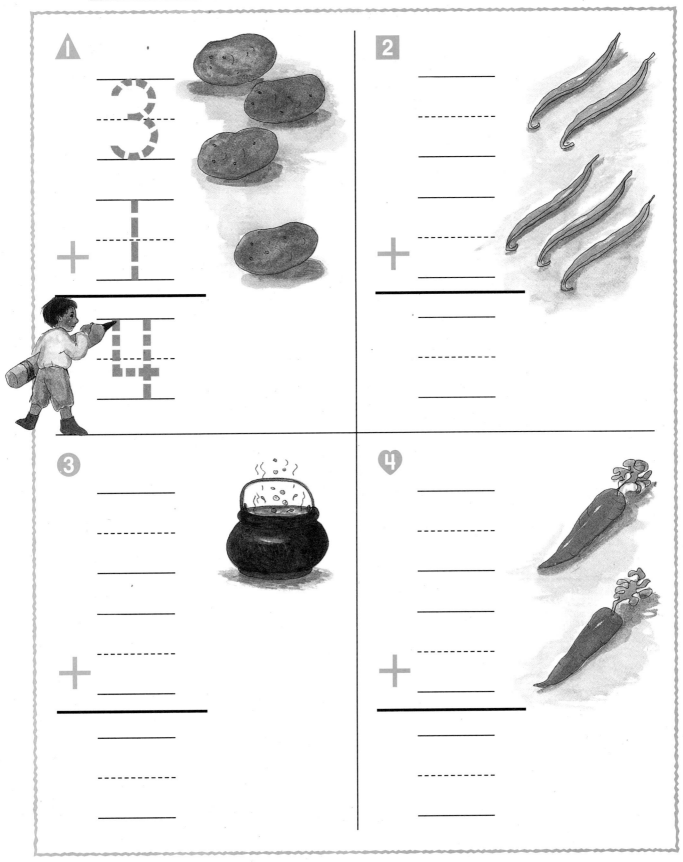

▲ 1

```
  3
+ 1
----
  4
```

2

```
____
____
+ ____
----
____
```

3

```
____
____
+ ____
----
____
```

4

```
____
____
+ ____
----
____
```

Directions Have children look at the pictures and then write the addition problems.

Home Connection Give your child four potatoes or carrots and help him or her create and write vertical addition problems.

I11

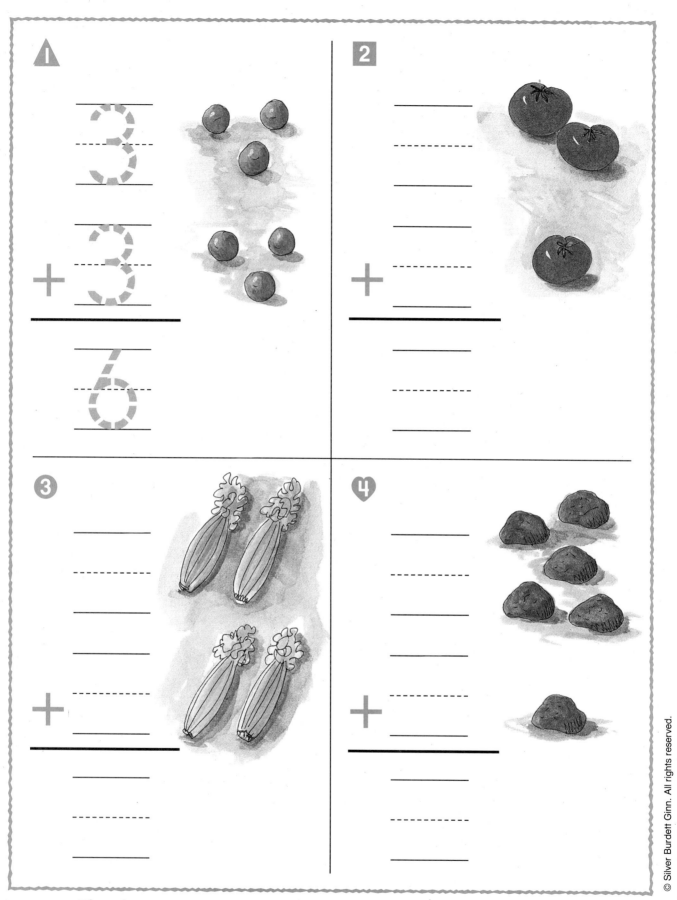

1

3
+ 3
———
6

2

3

4

Directions Have children look at the pictures and then write the addition problems.

I12

Name _____ **Adding Money**

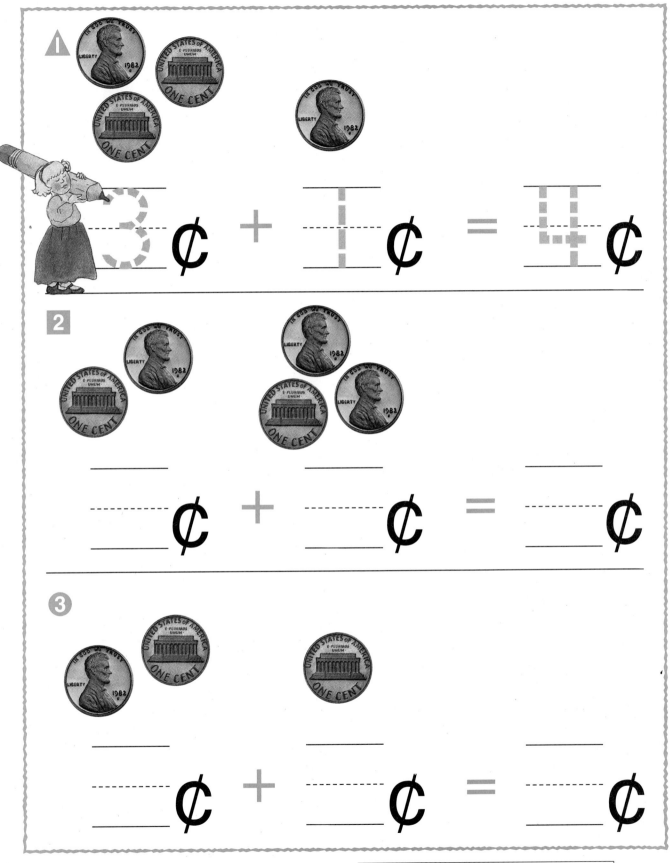

1. 3¢ + 1¢ = 4¢

2. ___¢ + ___¢ = ___¢

3. ___¢ + ___¢ = ___¢

Directions Have children look at the pennies and then write the addition sentences.

Home Connection Give your child five pennies. Have him or her create different addition problems with sums to 5.

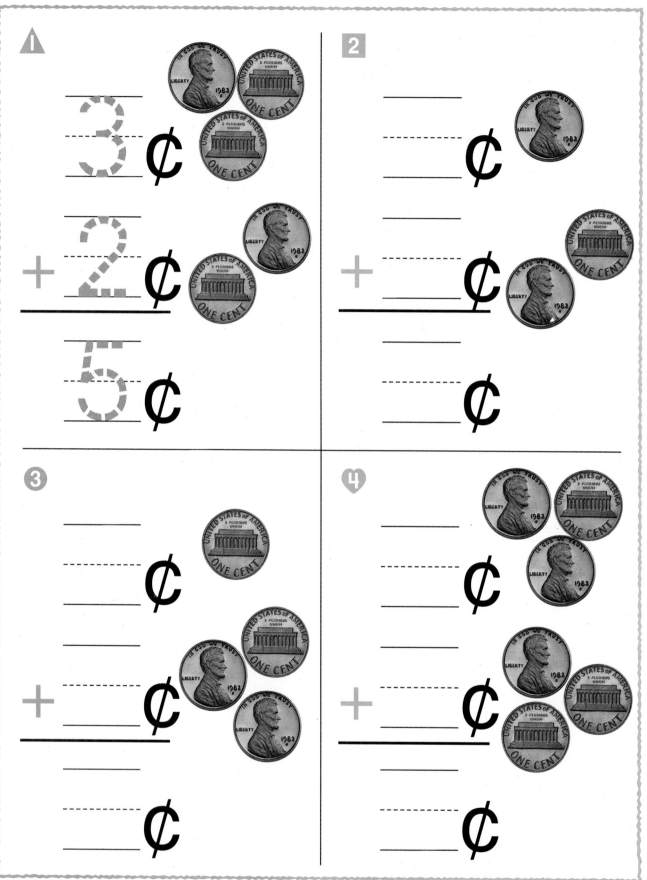

1.
3¢
+ 2¢
___
5¢

2.
___¢
+ ___¢
___
___¢

3.
___¢
+ ___¢
___
___¢

4.
___¢
+ ___¢
___
___¢

Directions Have children look at the pennies and then write the addition problems.

I14

Name _____

①

2

_____   _____   _____

- - - - - - -   **+**   - - - - - - -   **=**   - - - - - - -

_____   _____   _____

3 _____

- - - - - - -

_____

+ - - - - - - -

_____

_____

- - - - - - -

_____

❤ - - - - - - - **¢**

_____

+ - - - - - - - **¢**

_____

- - - - - - - **¢**

Directions Have children **1.** draw a picture to show 1 fish in the
pond and 3 more fish swimming to join it, **2.** write the addition
sentence, **3.** and **4.** write the addition problems.

Name _____

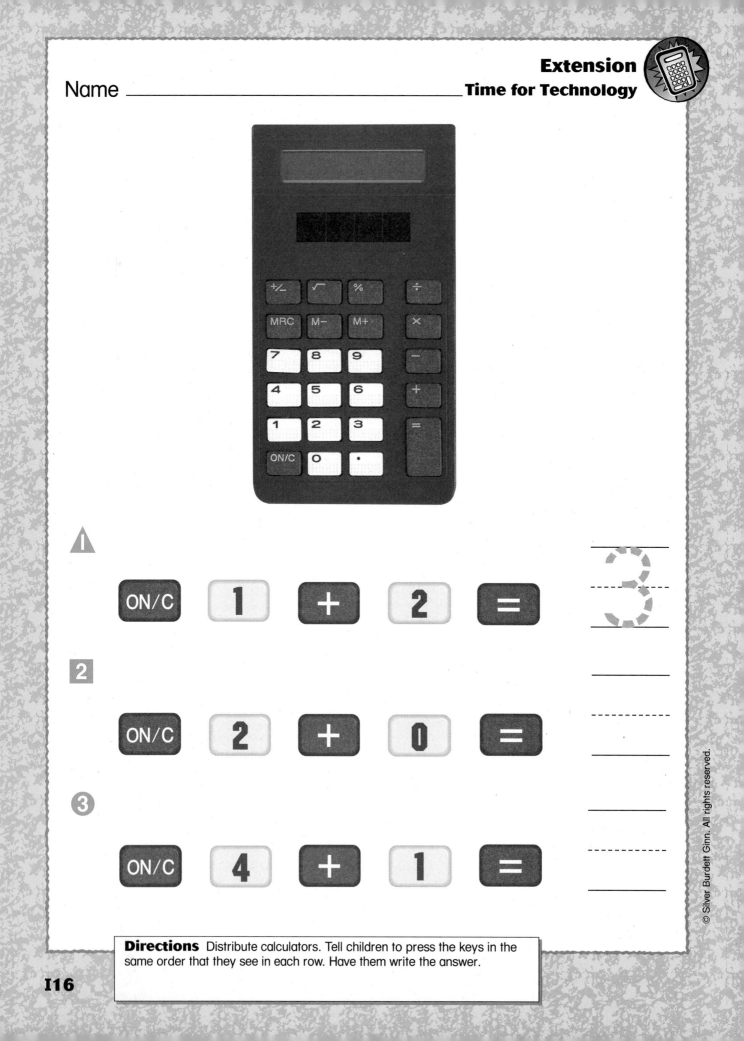

1 ON/C 1 + 2 = 3

2 ON/C 2 + 0 =

3 ON/C 4 + 1 =

Directions Distribute calculators. Tell children to press the keys in the same order that they see in each row. Have them write the answer.

I16

I'm a Farmer

A Note to the Family

During the next few weeks, your child will be learning about subtraction. Here are some learning ideas you can share together.

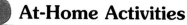 At-Home Activities

- Put six grapes or baby carrots on a plate, then either you or your child eats one. Ask your child how many are left. Continue the activity, eating one or more each time.

- Put six large seeds, such as pumpkin or sunflower seeds, in a row and invite your child to count them. Then remove two seeds and ask your child how many are left. You can continue by putting all six seeds back into a pile and then removing three (then four, then five).

Read About It!

To read more with your child about subtraction, look for these books in your local library.

- *3 Pandas Planting* by Megan Halsey (Bradbury Press, 1994)
- *Up to Ten and Down Again* by Lisa Campbell Ernst (Mulberry/Lothrop, Lee & Shepard, 1995)
- *Nine Ducks Nine* by Sarah Hayes (Candlewick, 1990)

Name _____

Problem-Solving

Act It Out

STRATEGY
Understand
Plan
Look Back
Solve

Directions Tell children the stories from Teacher Guide page 527. Have them use the cutouts to act out the problems.

Home Connection Have your child act out this problem, "You have four apples. I take away two. How many apples do you have left?"

J3

Directions Tell children the stories from Teacher Guide page 527. Have them use the cutouts to act out the problems.

J4

Name _____ **Using the Minus Sign**

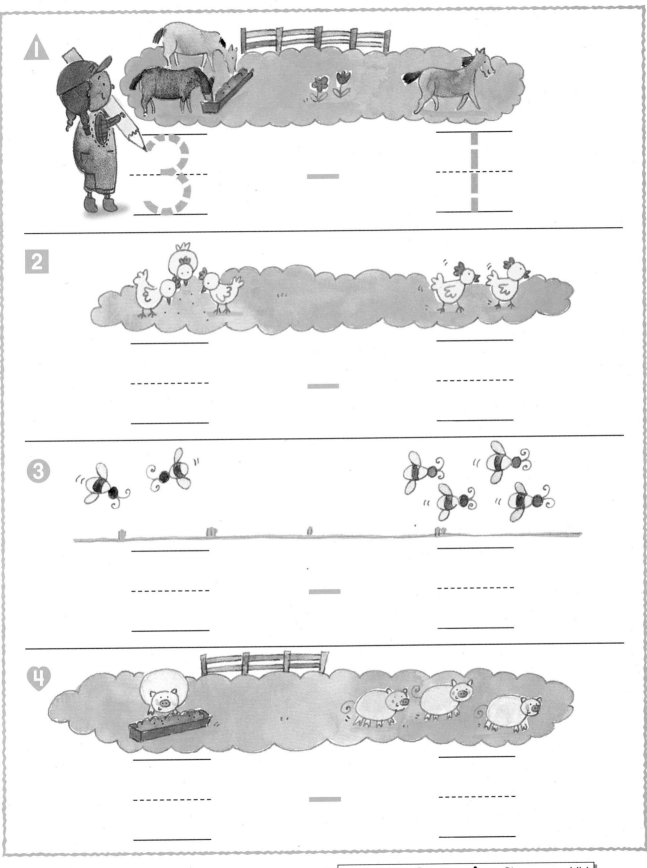

Directions Have children write how many there are in all and how many are leaving. Then have children tell how many are left.

Home Connection Show your child six eggs. Take away two eggs and ask your child how many are left.

J5

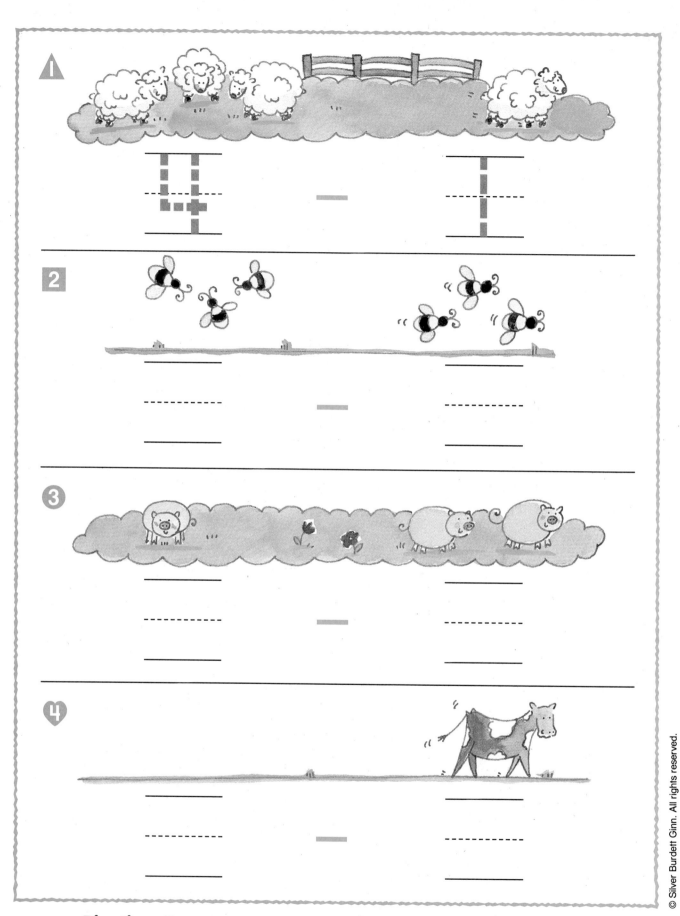

Directions Have children write how many there are in all and how many are leaving. Then have children tell how many are left.

J6

Name _____

1

$4 - 1 = 3$

2

$5 - 4 = $ _____

3

$2 - 2 = $ _____

4

$6 - 2 = $ _____

Directions Have children look at the pictures and then write how many are left.

Home Connection Have your child use the pictures to tell subtraction stories. For example, "I see four chickens. One walks away. Now three chickens are left."

J7

1 4 − 2 = 2

2 5 − 3 =

3 2 − 1 =

4 3 − 0 =

Directions Have children look at the pictures and then write how many are left.

INTERNET ACTIVITY
www.sbgmath.com

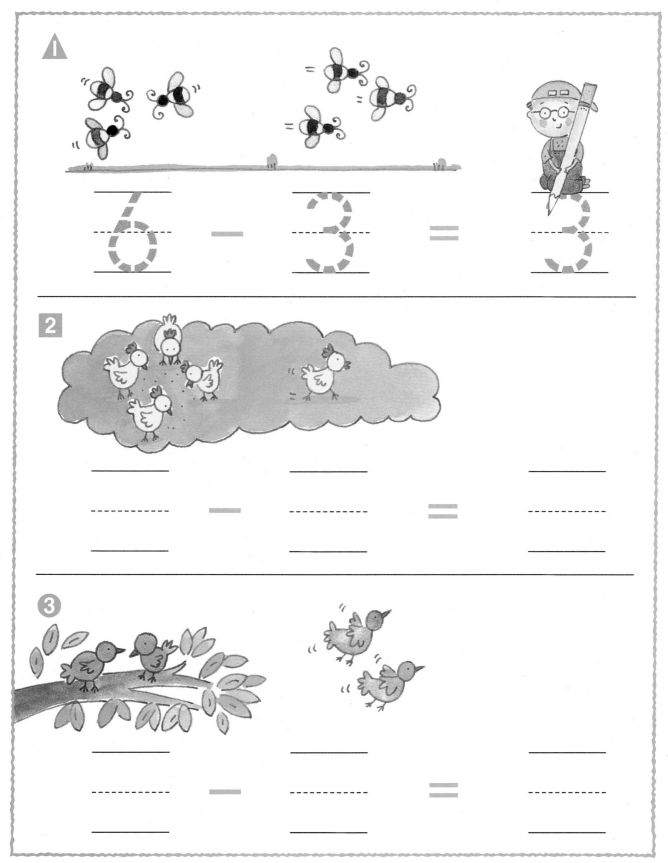

1.   6 - 3 = 3

2.   ___ ___ ___

     ---- - ---- = ----

     ___ ___ ___

3.   ___ ___ ___

     ---- - ---- = ----

     ___ ___ ___

Directions Have children look at the pictures and then write the subtraction sentences.

Home Connection Help your child draw a picture to show $4 - 2 = 2$.

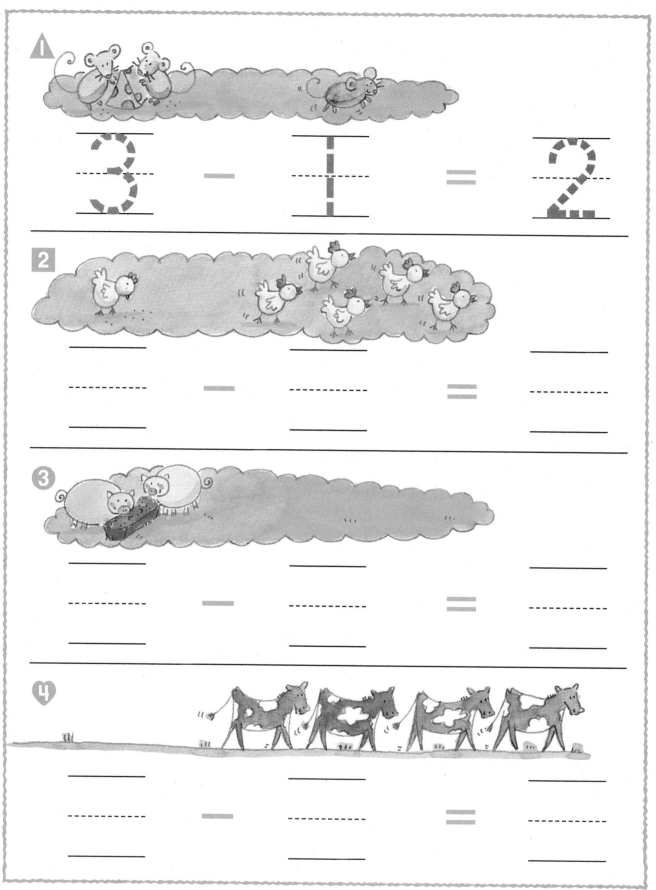

1 3 − 1 = 2

Directions Have children look at the pictures and then write the subtraction sentences.

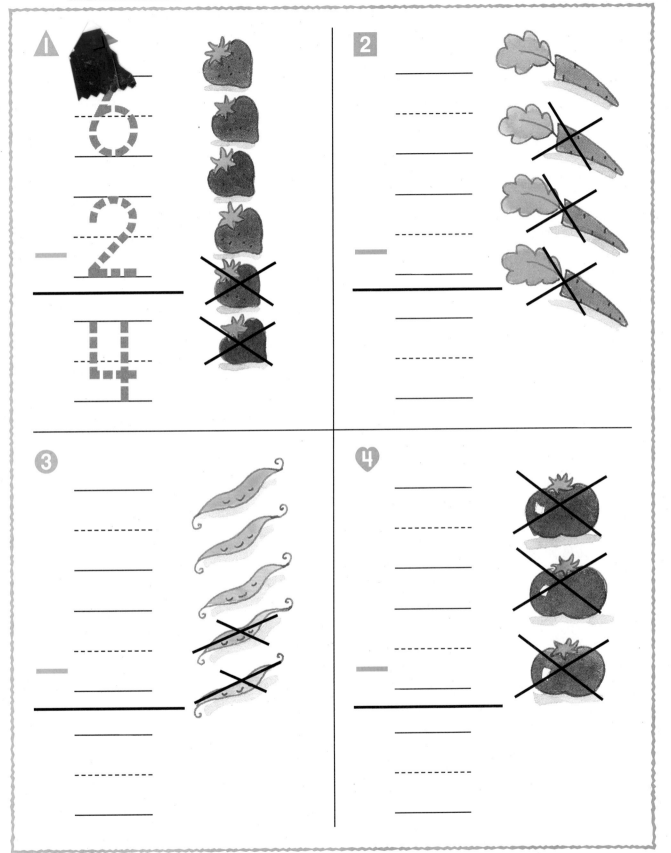

1

$$\begin{array}{r} 6 \\ -\ 2 \\ \hline 4 \end{array}$$

2

$$\begin{array}{r} \\ \underline{-} \\ \hline \end{array}$$

3

$$\begin{array}{r} \\ \underline{-} \\ \hline \end{array}$$

4

$$\begin{array}{r} \\ \underline{-} \\ \hline \end{array}$$

Directions Have children look at the pictures and then write the vertical subtraction problems.

Home Connection Have your child make up subtraction stories as you prepare a snack. For example, "I have 4 grapes. I eat 2. There are 2 grapes left."

J11

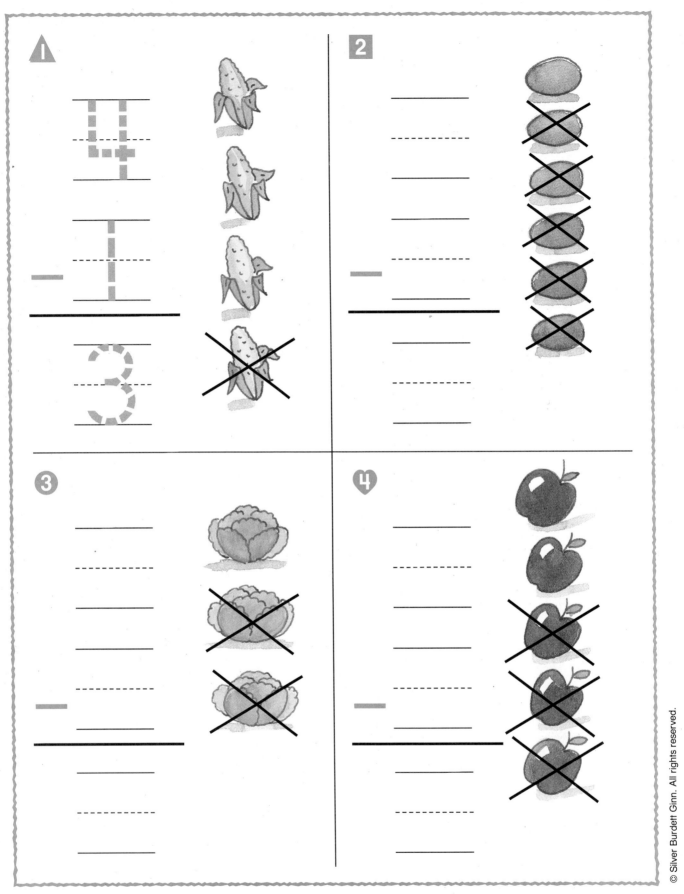

Directions Have children look at the pictures and then write the vertical subtraction problems.

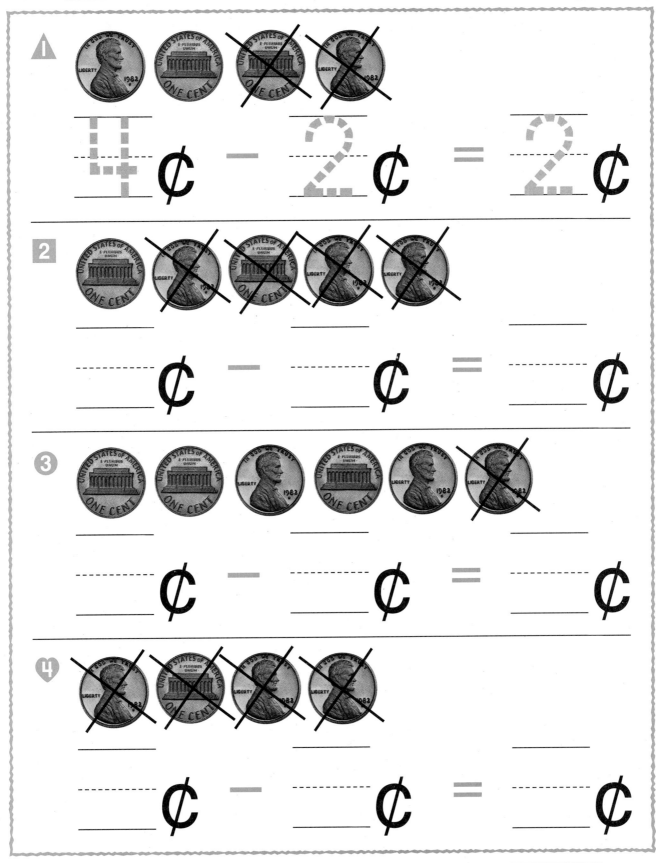

1 4 ¢ − 2 ¢ = 2 ¢

2 ___ ¢ − ___ ¢ = ___ ¢

3 ___ ¢ − ___ ¢ = ___ ¢

4 ___ ¢ − ___ ¢ = ___ ¢

Directions Have children look at the pennies and then write the subtraction sentences.

Home Connection Give your child four pennies. Help him or her create subtraction stories with them.

J13

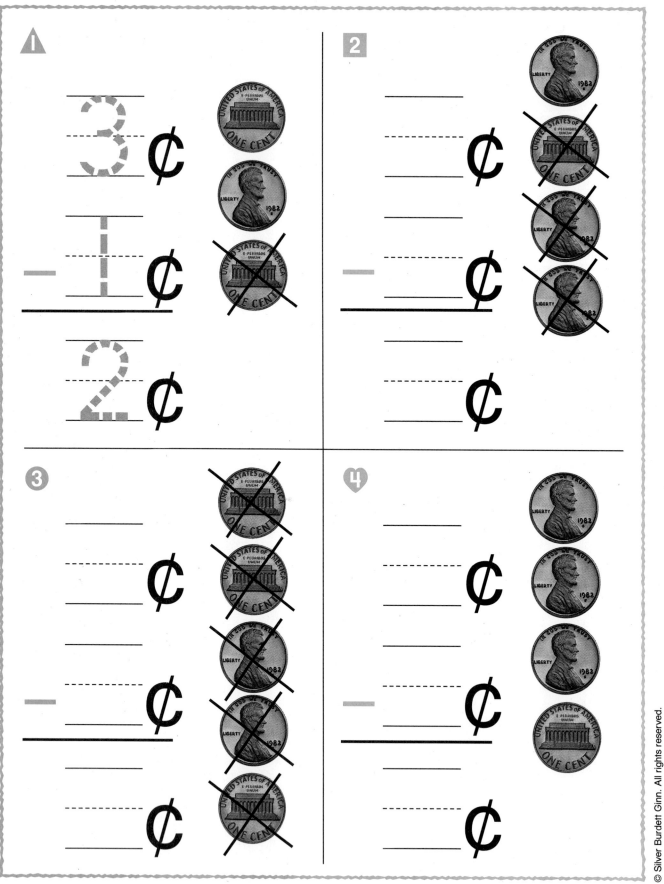

1

3 ¢

− 1 ¢

2 ¢

2

___ ¢

− ___ ¢

___ ¢

3

___ ¢

− ___ ¢

___ ¢

4

___ ¢

− ___ ¢

___ ¢

Directions Have children look at the pennies and then write the subtraction sentences.

Name _____ **Chapter Test**

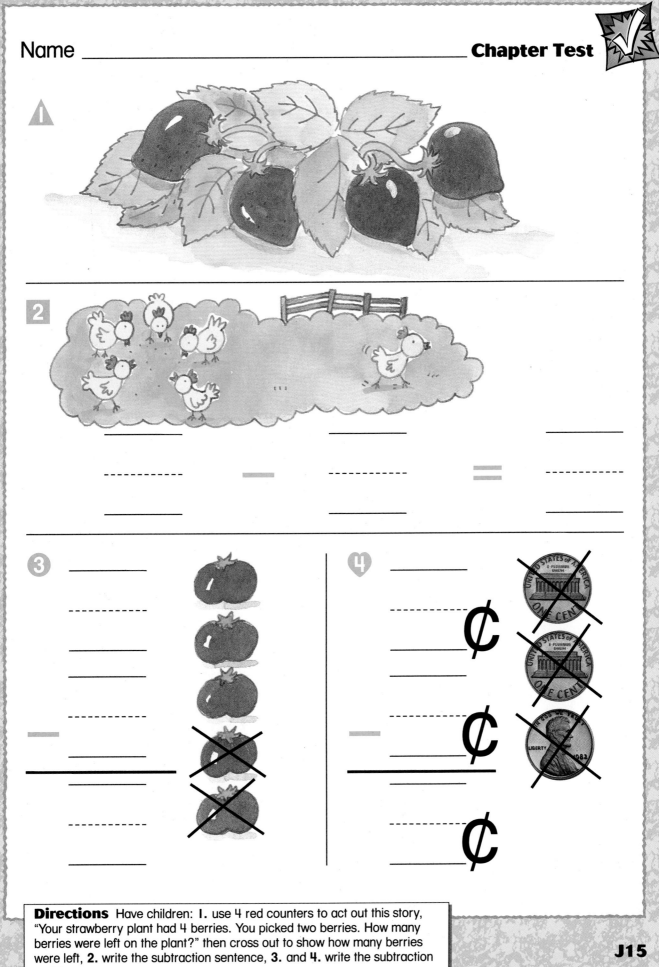

Directions Have children: **1.** use 4 red counters to act out this story, "Your strawberry plant had 4 berries. You picked two berries. How many berries were left on the plant?" then cross out to show how many berries were left, **2.** write the subtraction sentence, **3.** and **4.** write the subtraction problems.

Name _____

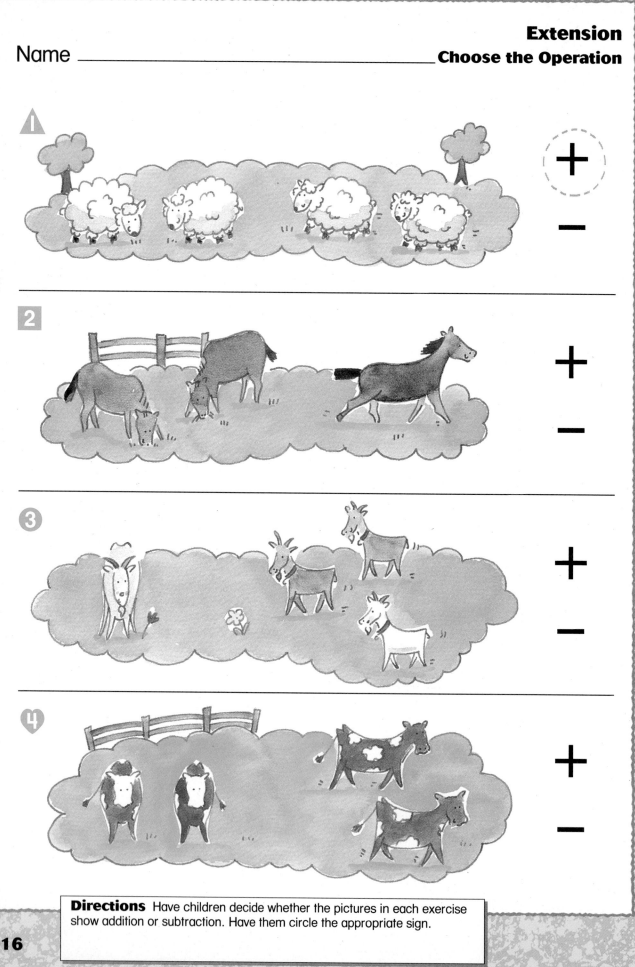

© Silver Burdett Ginn. All rights reserved.

Directions Have children decide whether the pictures in each exercise show addition or subtraction. Have them circle the appropriate sign.

J16